13 DANISH TALES

13 danish TALES

RETOLD BY
MARY C. HATCH

ILLUSTRATED BY EDGUN

HARCOURT, BRACE & WORLD, INC.
NEW YORK

CONTENTS

13 DANISH TALES

JAMES THE HUNTSMAN

ONCE upon a time there were two brothers. Their names were John and James, and their father had left them a house and garden to divide between them. But such a small house and garden, scarcely enough for one, to say nothing of two! And so John, who was the older brother, decided he should have the whole of it, and James, alas, had to go out into the world and seek his fortune as best he could.

The poor lad started early one morning and walked this way and that, but never a bit of a chance to make a fortune did he find, and when night came, he had to lie down on the bare earth with neither cover nor pillow to rest him.

"I don't know what's to become of me," he cried to himself. "I should like to be a huntsman, but where's to be found a horn, or a horse, or a hunting gun? Ah, me, I shall have to hire out as a farmhand and spend my days threshing grain and milking cows. A pretty job for a huntsman, I must say!"

And then he fell asleep, for though he was discouraged, he was sleepier still. But he got no more than forty winks, for suddenly he heard a little voice say, "Help me! Help me once, and I'll help you twice!" and he was up in a flash and looking around. Yet not a soul did he see. Then came that little voice again, "Help me! Help me once, and I'll help you twice!" and as it was close to the ground this time, he looked down carefully at his feet, and what should he see but a tiny little man no bigger than your finger.

"Now, to be sure, I'll help you if I can," said James. "What is your trouble, pray?"

"I am shut out of house and home," said the little man, "for I went to visit my grandfather in the hill yonder, and when I came back, there was a cow standing right over my doorway, and do what I will, she won't budge."

"Well, we'll soon remedy that," said James, and he ran over to the cow and chased her away.

" 'Tis a good deed you've done," said the little man. "And if you'll come back tomorrow sharp at the stroke of midnight, I'll be here to reward you."

"But I want nothing, sir," said James. "A good deed is its own reward."

"But it boils no potatoes for a hungry man," answered the dwarf. "Do as I say, and you will fare well." Then he took a hop, skip, and a jump

5

and was gone down a hole in the ground.

The next evening James returned to the hill, and straight on the dot of twelve, a curious thing happened. The hill rose up on four flaming red pillars, high enough for James to walk under, and there in the center stood the little dwarf.

"Welcome and more to my father's castle," said the dwarf, and he beckoned James inside. Then the pillars came down again, the hill closed round them, and James found himself inside the handsomest palace you ever dreamed of. The floors were of silver, the walls solid gold, and the lights all of glittering diamonds.

"Well!" said the little man. "Have you decided what shall be your reward?"

"Yes," said James, and he asked neither for money nor fame, but for the three things nearest and dearest to him—a horn, a horse, and a hunting gun.

"No sooner asked than gotten," said the dwarf, and he led James into a great room that was filled from top to bottom with nothing but

6

guns. There were guns big as trees and small as matchsticks, guns of iron and polished steel, guns of gold and silver, and guns never seen by ordinary mortals.

James looked at all this, and then walked over to a far corner where there hung a rusty old musket. "This one suits me best," he said. "I could not fire for the dazzle of the fancy fine ones."

"Very well," said the dwarf. "Take the rusty musket, and may it serve you well."

Then they went on to another room that was filled with horns from floor to ceiling, horns tall as a man and small as a pin, some tin and some brass, and some all aglitter with rubies and diamonds. "Well," said James, taking a long look around and resting his eyes on a plain little bugle that had been tossed into a far corner, "that little bugle is just the horn for me. I'd never sound a note for admiring the glitter of the fancy ones."

"Very well," said the dwarf. "Take your plain

little horn, and may it sound you well."

And then the little fellow led James to a great stable where there were arrayed the finest horses you ever laid eyes on, and some you've never seen, too, horses with wings, and horses with glowing eyes and fiery feet. But there was one plain horse also, a little gray creature with shaggy locks and knobby knees, and this one James chose. "He is just my speed," he said. "And he matches my horn and hunting gun, too."

"Very well," said the little man. "Take your plain little horse, and may he ride you well." And then there was a thunderous clap, and James found himself no longer in the brilliant palace stables, but outside on the cold, dark hillside. And he would have thought it all a dream, but there beside him stood the little horse, and there in his hand were the horn and the hunting gun.

Now he was a huntsman at last, so he mounted the horse, and away he galloped toward the king's palace. At the gates he was stopped by a guard. "What is your wish at the king's palace?" inquired the guard.

"I seek a place with the king's huntsmen," replied James.

The guard looked at James, at his rusty gun and battered horn, and he said with a laugh, "Well, you'll seek long and late, my lad. But try if you must. You'll find the chief huntsman yonder by the palace door."

"Thank you, I will seek him," said James, and so he went on through the palace grounds, and as he passed along an avenue of trees, a little bird flew down and lighted on his horn.

"Listen, listen," chirped the little bird. "You carry a wondrous horn and hunting gun, for whenever you blow your horn, all who hear it must dance, and wherever you point your gun, all will be killed."

"But I've no wish to kill anyone, nor yet to send people dancing in the street!" cried James.

"But thus you can serve the king," chirped the little bird. "Now listen, listen closely. The king's daughter and the prince she was to marry

9

were stolen a long time ago by the king of the dwarfs and carried away to the very hill where you were last night. Now listen, listen closely. If you can free them and return them safe and sound to the king, you will indeed be a great huntsman, and the king will give you half a kingdom or more."

"Well," said James, "I will do my best."

"Thank you," chirped the little bird. "And may you win well." Then up she flew back into the trees, and James rode on till he reached the head huntsman to whom he said boldly, "I seek a place with the king's huntsmen."

The head huntsman looked him up and he looked him down, and then he said with a laugh, "Well, you'll seek high and low, and long and late before you find a place with the king's huntsmen." Then off he rode, leaving poor James miserable and alone.

But a moment later, who should appear but the king himself, and when he saw the lad, he said, "What is your wish, my lad?"

"I wish to be one of your huntsmen," said James. "And I wish to rescue your daughter and the prince from the dwarf king."

"What strange wishes you have!" cried the king. "Do you not know my daughter was spirited away many years ago and neither hide nor hair have I seen of her since? Surely a poor fellow like you could never find her."

"I have a horse, a horn, and a hunting gun," said James. "And if you but follow me to the dwarf king's hill, I can prove my words."

"Very well," said the king, "for your eyes are kind and your hands are strong, and I can see you are no idle boaster." Then his horse was saddled, and the two of them set out for the dwarf king's palace. They arrived at the fateful hill close on to midnight, and James stopped at the foot and said, "First we must call out the dwarf king." Then he blew on his horn for the first time, a high shrill note, and as soon as the sound died away, there was a fearful blast from within the hill, and slowly it rose as before on

fiery red pillars, and inside, in a palace shining
like the sun, they saw the dwarf king. He was
a fearful-looking little troll, no taller than your
boot, with a nose as long as your arm, and eyes
big as saucers; and at sight of James and the
king, he began to howl most dolefully.

"It's little use crying will do you," said James,
"for 'tis the king's daughter you must serve up,
and all safe and sound, too."

At this the dwarf king howled louder than
ever. "Gold and silver you may have," he cried,
"but not the king's young daughter. She sings
sweet as a nightingale from morn till night, and
I'll not give her up."

"Well," said James, "we'll see about that,"
and once more he raised the horn to his lips.
This time he played a merry tune, one that was
made for dancing and it set the dwarf to kick-
ing his heels, round and round, till he was out
of breath and weak in the legs. Then over he fell
on the point of his nose, and round and round he
spun again till finally he had to cry, "Stop, stop!

I am a thousand years old, and you are shaking me to dust."

"Will you return my daughter, young and fair as when you stole her?" cried the king.

"Younger and fairer," shrieked the dwarf, and so James stopped the merry tune, and the troll stood upright again, and then rushed to the back of the palace and returned a moment later with the lovely princess. And indeed she did seem younger and fairer, for time means little in the dwarf king's mountain, and her father received her with welcome arms.

But what of the young prince without whom the princess would never be happy? "Where is the prince?" cried James. "Up with him quick, else you shall dance upon your nose again."

"But he is here no longer," said the dwarf king, and so James set about to play another merry tune, but at that moment there was a soft neighing, and looking up, the princess saw the little gray horse beside James.

"There is the prince," she cried. "He was

13

changed into a horse so we could not plot to run away together."

"Change him back into a man again," the king commanded the dwarf.

"On one condition," said the dwarf.

"What is the condition?" asked the king.

"Give me back my horn and gun," said the dwarf.

"Take them and gladly," exclaimed James, and he tossed them to the dwarf. Then the horse disappeared, and there stood before them the handsome young prince. And with a crash the hill closed in, and the four happy people were standing in a field a long way off, and the sun was rising in the east behind them.

"Well," said the king to James, "you have kept your promise, so I will keep mine, my lad. You shall rule half my country, and be a prince besides, with your own crown and throne."

"But I would be happy with less," said James. "I was never educated for court, being only a poor man's son."

"Never mind the education," said the king. "Truth to tell, you needn't know much to wear a crown and sit on a throne. Just keep your shoulders back and head up. No one likes a slouchy prince."

"That is true," said the princess.

"True indeed," said the prince.

And so there was nothing for James to do but become a prince, too. And everyone lived happily ever after—all but the king's huntsmen. They all died of envy shortly afterwards, every single one of them.

THE TALKING POT

ONCE upon a time there was a man so poor that he had nothing in the world but a wife, a house, and one lone cow. And after a time, he got even poorer than that, and so he had to take the cow to market and sell her.

On the way he met a fine-faced stranger.

16

"Well, my good man," said the stranger, "whither away with that fat cow?"

"To market, and thank you," said the man, though the cow was far from fat.

"Then perhaps you will sell her to me," said the stranger.

Yes, the farmer would sell and gladly, provided the price were twenty dollars or more.

The stranger shook his head. "Money I cannot give you," he said. "But I have a wonderful pot that I will trade you," and he showed the farmer a three-legged iron pot with a handle that was tucked under his arm.

Now, truth to tell, there was nothing at all wonderful-looking about the pot, and it might have hung in any chimney in the country. Besides, the poor man had nothing to put in it, neither food nor drink, so he declined to make the trade. "Money I need, and money I must have," he said, "so you may keep your wonderful pot."

But hardly had he said these words than the

pot began to speak. "Take me, take me," cried the pot, "and you'll never have cause to rue it." And so the man changed his mind and made the trade, for if the pot could talk, then surely it could do other things, too.

Home he now returned, and when he reached there, he hid the pot in the stable where the cow had always been kept, for he wanted to surprise his wife. Then he went inside. "Well, good wife," he said, "fetch me a bit to eat and a sup to drink, for I've walked a long mile and back today."

But his wife would do none of it till she heard about her husband's success at the market. "Did you make a fine bargain?" she asked.

"Fine as fine," said her husband.

"That is well," nodded the wife, "for we've a hundred places to use the money."

But it wasn't a money bargain. No indeed, exclaimed her husband.

Not a money bargain! Well, pray then, what had the good man gotten for the cow, cried the wife, and she would not rest till her husband had taken her to the barn and showed her the three-legged pot tied up to the stall.

And then the good wife *was* angry! Trading a fine, fat cow—though truth to tell it was neither fine nor fat—for a common black pot that might hang in anyone's chimney.

"You are stupid as a goose," cried the wife. "Now what will we do for food and drink? If you were not so tough, I do believe I would stew you!" And she started to shake her husband. But before she could do the poor man much damage, the pot began to speak again.

"Clean me, and shine me, and put me on the fire," said the pot, and at that the woman sang a different tune. "Well!" she said. "If you can talk, perhaps you can do other things, too." And she took the pot and scrubbed it and polished it, and then hung it over the fire.

"I will skip, I will skip," said the pot.

"How far will you skip?" asked the woman.

"Up the hill, and down the dale, and into the

rich man's house," cried the little pot, and with that, it jumped down from the hook, and skipping across the room, went out the door, and up the road to the rich man's house. Here the rich man's wife was making fine cakes and puddings, and the pot jumped up on the table and settled there still as a statue.

"Well!" exclaimed the rich man's wife. "You are just what I need for my finest pudding." Then she stirred in sugar and spices, and raisins and nuts, a whole host of good things, and the pot took them all without a murmur. In a few minutes, the pudding was made, and the woman picked up the pot and put it on the fire. But down the pot jumped and skipped to the door.

"Dear me," exclaimed the woman. "What are you doing, and where are you going?"

"I'm bound for home to the poor man's house," cried the little pot, and away it went skipping up the road till it was back at the poor man's little cottage.

When the couple saw that the pot had brought

them a fine pudding, the finest they had ever seen, they were very pleased, and the farmer said, "Now, my good wife, did I not make a good bargain when I traded our poor old cow for this wonderful pot?"

"Indeed you did," said his wife, and she fell to eating the pot's fine pudding.

The next morning, the pot again cried, "I will skip, I will skip!" And the wife said, "How far will you skip?"

"Up hill and down dale, and into the rich man's barn," the little pot replied, and out the house and up the road it went skipping, straight to the rich man's barn.

The rich man's servants were threshing grain, and the pot skipped to the center of the floor and stood there still as a statue.

"Well!" said one of the threshers. "Here is just the pot to hold a bushel of grain," and he poured in a sackful. But this took up no room at all, and so he poured in another and another till there was not a grain of anything left in the whole barn.

"A most peculiar pot!" exclaimed the men. "Though it looks as if it had hung in any number of chimneys." And then they tried to lift it, but it slid away from them and went skipping across the floor.

"Dear me," cried the men. "What are you doing, and where are you going?"

"I'm bound for home to the poor man's house," said the pot, and out the door it skipped, and though the men ran after it, they were left huffing and puffing far behind.

When the little pot reached home again, it poured out the wheat in the poor man's barn, and there was enough to make bread and cakes for years to come.

But that was not the end of its good deeds, for on the third morning it said again, "I will skip, I will skip!" And the old wife asked, "Where will you skip?" And it answered, "Up hill and down dale to the rich man's house," and out the house it ran at once.

Now the rich man was in his counting house counting out his money, and when the little pot arrived, up it jumped on the table, right in the midst of all the gold pieces.

"What a fine pot," cried the rich man. "Just the thing for my money." And into the pot he tossed handful after handful of money till not one piece was left loose on the table. Then he picked up his treasure to hide it in his money cupboard, but the pot slipped from his fingers and hopped to the door.

"Stop, stop," cried the rich man. "You have all my money."

"But not yours for long," said the pot. "I carry it home to the poor man's house," and out the room it skipped and back to the poor man's cottage. There it poured out the golden treasure, and the old couple cried aloud with delight.

"Now you have enough," said the pot, and indeed they did, enough and more, too, and so the wife washed the pot carefully and put it aside.

But in the morning, the pot was off again, straight for the rich man's house, and when the rich man saw it, he cried, "There is the wicked pot that stole my wife's pudding, and my wheat, and all my gold. But it shall bring everything back, every last farthing and more." Then he grabbed the pot, but bless my soul, if he didn't stick fast! And though he tugged and he pulled, he couldn't get free.

"I will skip, I will skip," said the pot.

"Well, skip to the North Pole," cried the man, still furiously trying to free himself, and at that, away went the pot and the man with it. Up the hill they waltzed and down the hill, and never once did they stop, not even to say hello or good-bye at the old couple's cottage, for the pot was in a great hurry. The North Pole, you know, is far, far away, even for a fast-skipping pot.

MOTHER'S PET

ONCE upon a time, a poor man and his wife had three sons. Now the two older ones were strong and handsome as the day is long, but the youngest was a puny lad who neither worked nor played, but stayed at home all day round his mother's skirts. He was called Mother's Pet, and when, at length, the parents died, and the eldest son took the house and the second son took the farm, he was left with nothing at all.

But this he considered quite unfair, and when he complained about it, the eldest brother said, " 'Tis unfair indeed, my boy, and so you shall have your mother's kneading trough. Then if you are clever enough to find flour and yeast, you can make cakes and cookies all day long, and live like a king."

And so Mother's Pet received the kneading trough, and though 'twas little enough, it was better than nothing, and with it, the lad made a boat and set sail to seek his fortune.

After many a long day on the sea, he reached a far kingdom, and here he sought service with the king.

"What is your name, and what can you do?" asked the king.

"My name is Mother's Pet, and I can do this and that," answered the lad.

"Well," said the king, "we've no this and that around, and besides, you're so small a good sneeze would blow you away."

26

"True," said the lad, "but I'm quick, and a little fellow can squeeze in and out where a big fellow would get stuck fast."

This the king could not deny, and so he gave the boy a place in the kitchen where a light-footed lad was needed, and though the boy had his eyes on something that paid more—admiral, or general, or prime minister—still a kitchen was not at all a bad place. There one got chicken breasts and jelly tarts by the score; and plenty of state secrets were served up, too.

Now the king had a daughter as pretty as a picture, and she was sought by every prince and duke in the country. But she, alas, loved none of them, and so they wearied her no end, and she tried many a scheme to get rid of them, but not a one succeeded.

Finally word of her plight reached the kitchen, and though the kitchen maids thought she was very foolish, for they themselves would have been only too happy to marry a prince, or a duke, or even an ordinary man, Mother's Pet quite sympathized with her.

"How dull for the princess to hear nothing but flattery and sweet words from morn till night," he said. "Now I am just the man to help her out."

And so one day he invited the princess to the kitchen. "Dear princess," he said, "shall I tell you how to get rid of your suitors?"

"Dear kitchen lad," said the princess, "please do tell me, and if you are successful, you shall be chief tart maker in the kingdom."

"Very well," said the lad, "for I am most fond of tarts. Now listen well, and mark my words. Over the sea and far away are a hen that lays a golden egg a day, a golden mill that grinds by itself, and a lantern of gold that can shed light and learning over the whole kingdom. Now you must send your suitors on a quest for these, and you must promise to marry the one who returns with them first—though you need not worry about that, for 'twill be many a long year before any of them return."

"Thank you, dear lad," said the princess. "You are clever indeed." Then she called all the dukes and princes to her. "Dear suitors," she said, "I cannot decide which among you I should marry, so I shall put you to a test. Over the sea and far away are a hen that lays a golden egg a day, a golden mill that grinds by itself, and a lantern of gold that can shed light and learning over the whole kingdom. Whoever wishes to gain my hand must go in search of these, and the one who returns home with them shall have me for his bride."

Well, what a rush out the door there was! Hardly any of the suitors stopped even for lunch or luggage, and in a few minutes the palace was completely deserted.

All now went well for a year and a day. Then, as not a single, solitary man had returned home, the king became alarmed, for the princess was getting no younger fast, and the king wanted no old maids on his throne.

"Daughter," he cried, "who advised you to

send your suitors in search of a hen that lays a golden egg a day, and a golden mill that grinds by itself, and a lantern of gold that can shed light and learning over the whole kingdom?"

"A clever kitchen lad advised me," said the princess. "And he advised me well."

"We shall see about that," said the king, and he called the lad to him. "Well, my boy," said the king, "you sent all the princes and dukes of the kingdom on a merry chase, and now I shall send you tripping, too. You must go in search of the hen that lays a golden egg a day, and the golden mill that grinds by itself, and the lantern of gold that can shed light and learning over the whole kingdom, and if you do not return with them, then you shall lose your head."

Now the lad had no desire to lose his head, so he said very well to the king, though how to get the treasures was something of a problem. He knew where to find them right enough, for his mother had told him, and her mother had told her, and her mother had told her. They were kept by an old troll and his wife who lived west by the sea at the end of the world. But stealing the treasures from under their noses was quite another task.

Yet try the lad must, so he climbed into his faithful kneading trough and set sail for the troll's domain. And as the sea was smooth and the wind kind, he reached there in a week or so. Then he hid by the shore till it was quite dark and he could tiptoe unseen up to the house and take a peek inside. And here he saw, up under the roof, the hen that laid the golden egg, and down below, the golden mill that ground by itself, and the lantern that could shed light and learning over the whole kingdom.

And here, too, were the old troll and his wife, but luckily they were dead to the world with snoring and dreaming, and so the lad climbed up to the roof and let himself down through a little trap door that opened right above the famous hen.

Then he threw his cap over the hen and

climbed back out again, and went racing toward the sea. But the hen had something to say about such treatment, and she set up such a clucking and crowing that the old troll and his wife were awakened and ran after Mother's Pet.

"Stop, thief, stop!" cried the old troll as he huffed and puffed along.

"Not till I'm home safe and sound," called back the lad.

"I'll eat you alive," screamed the troll.

"Not till you catch me," called back the lad, and on he ran. And he kept far ahead, for he was so small that the wind tumbled him along, and by the time the trolls were down to the shore, he was in his boat and far out to sea.

When the lad reached home again, there was great excitement over the magic hen, and the king took the boy out of the kitchen and made him a duke. But this was a dull life, and besides, he had not finished his quest, so in a few days he set out again to try his luck with the mill and the lantern.

The sea was fair and the wind kind, and he was not long in reaching the troll's land a second time. Here he hid down by the shore till it was pitch black and nigh onto midnight. Then he tiptoed up to the troll's house and peeked inside. And there on the table were the mill and the lantern, and there beside them were the troll and his wife. But fortunately they were dead to the world with snoring and dreaming, and so in the lad crept.

Now he had armed himself with a heavy club, and hiding behind the bed, he reached up and gave the old troll such a blow on the big toe that he awakened and jumped out of bed with a scream. "Well, old woman!" he cried to his wife, for he thought she had struck him, "I'll teach you to mistreat a poor sleeping man," and out of the bed he threw her.

This of course angered the old woman, and so they fell to fighting, throwing their fists about and rocking the house with their yelling. And while they traded blows, Mother's Pet seized the mill and the lantern and went flying back toward his boat. But the lantern blinked so brightly that it soon caught the attention of the trolls, and then they stopped fighting and ran after the lad.

But though they ran fast, Mother's Pet ran even faster, for he was so light he flew on the wind, and by the time they reached the shore, he was already in his boat.

" 'Tis foolish things you have stolen," cried the troll, "and worth nothing at all."

"Then we are even," laughed the lad, "for I've given you nothing for them."

"If you'll come back," cried the troll, "I'll make you a worthy gift."

"And I'll be back," answered the boy, "when the sea becomes a mountain." And with that he set off for home.

But the trolls were not to let him off so easily.

"Let us empty the sea and make a mountain now," cried the old woman, and her man agreed, and so they both knelt down and began to drink with might and main.

They drank and drank till they were puffed out like balloons, and they drank so fast that the waves rose high as mountains, and Mother's Pet in his little boat was spun round and swept back to the shore, right to the trolls' mouths.

And that would have been the end of the poor lad, but just at that moment, the troll and his wife took one gulp too much, and POP, they burst into a million pieces. Then the water poured back into the sea, and it made such a splash that the lad was thrown clear across the sea from the end of the world back to his own shore. And here the king and the princess were waiting for him, and when they saw the wonderful mill and the lantern of gold, the king promoted the lad from duke to prince at once.

But this was a dull life, too, so the lad proposed to the princess, and she accepted quite willingly, and they were married with much fanciness and finery.

And everyone lived happily ever after, for the

hen laid so many golden eggs that no one had to pay taxes, and the mill ground out food and clothes for everyone, and the lantern shed so much light and learning that no one ever had to go to school any more. And this, of course, was the best of all—at any rate, that is what the children thought.

THE FOOLISH LAD

ONCE there was a woman who had an only son, and this lad, according to everyone, was quite a dunce. Now, one day, when the woman had been churning and had made a fine roll of butter, the boy said, "Let me take the butter to town and sell it." But his mother answered, "No indeed, son," for he had never been to town before. The boy coaxed and pleaded so

37

long, however, that finally his mother consented, and giving him the butter, sent him on his way.

The boy trudged along till he reached a large rock. This he thought was the town, so he said to it, speaking very politely, "Would you like to buy some butter?"

Now of course the rock made no answer, so the lad went on talking. "I can tell you," he said, "that my butter is very good. If you wish, you may have a taste of it." Then, without waiting for permission, he smeared a bit of butter on the stone, and as the day was very warm, it soon melted and disappeared.

"Well, my good town," said the boy, "I see that you like the butter very much. You may as well buy it all, and if you haven't the money today, you can pay me tomorrow." Then he smeared on the rest of the butter and returned home.

When his mother saw him, she exclaimed, "How quickly you sold the butter, my son. Who bought it, and for how much?"

"I sold it to the town, and he will pay me to-morrow."

"You sold it to the town?" cried his mother. "Why, that's nonsense!"

"Indeed it is not," said the boy. "It is exactly what you told me to do."

"Very well," said his mother. "But it makes neither rhyme nor reason to me, and another time I will think twice before letting you make off with my fine butter."

Next day the boy wanted to go and collect his money. "But it will be of no use," said his mother. "You will get nothing."

The boy would not listen to her, however, and went of his own accord to the stone. "I have come to collect the money for the butter that you bought from me yesterday," he said politely.

The rock, of course, did not utter a single word, and this made the boy angry. "You wretch," he cried. "Yesterday you bought my butter, and today you refuse to pay for it. You won't even answer me. Well, I will show you that I'm not to be trifled with." And he took hold of the rock and kicked and tugged at it until it rolled over. Underneath, lo and behold, he found a whole pot full of money, and as he was sure it was the money due him, he picked it up without hesitating a moment and hurried home with it.

When his mother saw him, she was very much surprised. "Where did you get so much money?" she cried.

"From the town, of course," answered the boy. "It made me angry for it wouldn't speak to me, and it wouldn't pay me, so I turned it over and took all the money."

"I don't understand your foolish talk," cried his mother. "But never mind. You have made a great deal of money, and that is the important thing." Then she put the money away, and no more was said of the matter.

Sometime later the woman killed her cow. Then the boy said, "Let me take the meat to town and sell it." And since he had done so well with the butter, his mother consented, and putting a large piece in a basket, sent him on his way.

This time he really reached the town, and he walked up and down, having a good look at things, until he met several dogs. The dogs barked at him, and so he said, "How do you do? Would you like to buy some meat?"

The dogs barked again.

"Very well, then," said the lad. "You may sample it."

But the dogs wanted more than a sample, so the boy threw the entire piece to them. "Eat it all," he said, "and tomorrow I will come for the money."

The next day he was there bright and early. But the dogs gave him no money, only barked and barked.

"Are you refusing to pay me?" cried the boy. "Then indeed, I will teach you manners." And he picked up the dog with the finest collar, squeezed it under his arm, and started out for the king's palace.

When he arrived there, however, he was stopped by one of the king's guards who forbade him to enter. "But I have been cheated, and I need the king's help," cried the boy.

"Well," said the guard, "what is your trouble?"

The boy then told him what the dogs had done, and when the guard had heard the story through, he said, "This is really a sad state of affairs, so I will let you pass to see the king. But first you must promise to pay me half of what you receive for the meat."

The lad promised, and the guard let him by. But soon he was stopped by another guard, and he had to promise this fellow half of what he received, too. Finally he reached the king's rooms, however, and his presence was announced. The king appeared, and the boy told him what villains the dogs had been.

But the king had no sympathy for him. He merely shrugged his shoulders and said, "I can't help you. If you have sold the meat to the dogs, you must get your money where you can and when you can."

"Very well," said the boy. "I will start with this dog's hide," and he caught hold of the creature's collar and gave him a thorough shaking.

Now you must know that the king had a very beautiful daughter who, alas, was always sad and tearful. This made the king very unhappy, and he had declared that whoever was able to cheer her and make her laugh should marry her and have half the kingdom. Today, as luck would have it, the princess happened to overhear the lad tell his story to the king, and when it was finished, she thought it so funny that she laughed and laughed and could not stop herself.

The king was mightily pleased to see his daughter laughing once more. "Well, my lad," he exclaimed to the boy, "matters are quite different now, and your meat will indeed sell high, for you can marry my daughter."

"But I don't care for her," said the lad.

"What a strange way to feel!" said the king. "But it quite suits me, for I would rather not have you marry her. I will give you a bag of dollars instead."

"I don't care for money either," said the lad.

"And that is stranger still!" exclaimed the king. "But never mind. What would you like to have?"

"I want sixty lashes, no more and no less," declared the boy.

This seemed a poor reward to the king, but as it was the boy's wish, he called his men to him and said, "Give this boy sixty lashes."

"No, thank you," said the lad. "You must give them to the guards. They made me promise to give them each half of what was paid for the meat, and I cannot go back on my word."

The king's men hurried out to pay the guards, and the king turned to the boy. "Now, my lad," he said, "I am sure you are not so foolish as you seem. Would you not like to marry my daughter?"

Indeed the boy would, and so he and the princess were wed, and they lived long and happily together. And though I may be wrong, it seems to me that for a dunce, this boy did very well.

MISTRESS GOOD LUCK
AND DAME KNOW-ALL

ONE day two old crones met on the highway. They were Mistress Good Luck and Dame Know-All, and as they walked along together, Mistress Good Luck said to the other, "Which do you think is better, good luck or great learning?"

"To be sure, and it's great learning," said

Dame Know-All, but of course Mistress Good Luck did not agree with her, and so they fell to arguing about the matter, and they argued this way and that till they came to a field where a young lad was plowing.

Then Mistress Good Luck said, "Dear Dame Know-All, please wish a wish upon the head of the boy we see plowing yonder, and give him great learning and great wisdom. But luck he shall have none of, and then we will see which 'tis better to have, a bit of luck or a bit of learning."

"Very well," said Dame Know-All, and so she wished a wish upon the boy's head, and gave him wisdom and knowledge enough 'twould have made your head ache to carry it. Then she and Mistress Good Luck moved on their way, and the lad went on with his plowing.

But not for long did he plow, for soon he began to feel how clever and wise he was, and after a short while, he threw down his reins and exclaimed, "I am so wise that there is nothing in the world I do not know, and now I am going to town and make myself a fortune." And there and then he skipped out of the field and started on his way.

When he arrived in town, he decided that he would like to be a watchmaker, so he went to the royal watchmaker and asked for a place in his shop. But this worthy man said nay, for the boy's fingers looked rough and clumsy, and besides, he was sure to have an enormous appetite and eat everyone out of house and home.

But the young man begged and begged, giving weight to his words with money, and so the watchmaker finally changed his mind, and the boy was given a place in the shop.

Not long after this, the king sent for the royal watchmaker. "My good man," he said, "I want you to make me a wondrous clock. It must walk about by itself, and when I sit on my throne and say, 'Here sits your great and loving majesty,' it is to stop in front of me and bow low."

"But your majesty!" cried the royal watchmaker. "Such a clock can never be made."

"If it is what the king wishes, it can be done," said his royal highness. "And if you lack fingers nimble enough or a head clever enough for the task, then we shall find another watchmaker to fill your shoes." And with that, the king walked haughtily away.

Now the poor man was so upset by this order that he could neither sleep nor eat, and finally the young apprentice said, "Master, if you will but give me leave, I can make the king's clock just as he wishes, and better, too."

But the master would have none of it. "Away with your nonsense," he cried. " 'Tis I who must make the clock."

Still not one spring of it got put together, and so the apprentice said a second time, "Master, if you will but give me leave, I can make the king's clock just as he wishes, and better, too."

But again the master refused him, and gave him a resounding box on the ears. Still not a spring got made, and so the boy said a third time,

"Master, if you will but give me leave, I can make the king's clock just as he wishes, and better, too."

And this time the master gave leave, and what is more, the lad was allowed to work in a room of his own, and he could come and go when and how he pleased.

Now a month and a day went by in this fashion, and then the master paid the lad a call to see how the clock was progressing. But not a bit of it was to be seen anywhere! Instead, the walls were covered from top to bottom with drawings that were strange and curious.

"A fine state of affairs, I must say," cried the master. "You beg and you promise, but not one spring of a clock do I see!"

"Well, you'll see it soon enough," said the boy. " 'Tis the plans, and good plans indeed, that I've drawn on the wall. Just leave me to work in peace and quiet, master."

And so the master left the boy to his work, and another month and a day went by. Then the master called on the lad again, and this time the room was heaped with wheels and cogs and cogs and wheels, all of a strange and curious size. But not a bit of a clock was to be seen anywhere!

"What a rascal you are," cried the master. "Here you beg and you promise, but never a clock do you make."

"Never fear," said the lad. "You shall have your clock before you know it. These are the works, and fine works, too, that you see here. Just leave me to work in peace and quiet, master."

And so the master left him, and sure enough, before he knew it, the clock *was* ready, and set upon his table to prove its excellence. And excellent it was, and wondrous, too. The master played that he was the king, and as the clock walked about, he said to it, "Here sits your great and loving majesty," and the clock stopped in front of him and bowed as prettily as a young page, and then beat out the time.

"What a wonderful, wonderful clock," cried

the master. "If I had not seen that it was made all of steel inside, I would say it had a real live head and a real warm heart. Walk and tick and bow again, little jewel of a clock." And so the wondrous clock was obliged to amuse the watchmaker and the apprentices for several long hours.

Shortly thereafter, the king sent for the clock, and so the royal watchmaker and the young apprentice took it to the palace, and it was tried out before the whole court, from the king and queen down to the least important noble. And so well did it perform, walking and ticking and daintily bowing, that the king was ready to burst with pleasure.

"What did I tell you?" he cried to the master. "A real royal watchmaker can make a real royal clock if he is really a royal watchmaker!"

Then the master had to confess that 'twas not he, but the apprentice lad who had constructed the wondrous clock that could walk, and tick, and bow like a man.

"Well," said the king, "a lad with such a

clever head needn't stay an apprentice for long."
And there and then he made the boy a page in
the palace.

Now you must know that this same king had
a daughter, and the cat had got her tougue as
the old saying goes, and no one could persuade
her to open her mouth and say a word. This distressed her father no end, for though a talking
woman is sometimes a nuisance, a silent one is
even worse, and one never knows yea or nay if
he's pleased her. And so the king was bound and
determined to cure the lass, and he proclaimed
far and wide that if anyone could make her talk,
the princess would be his, and half the kingdom,
too. But he wanted no halfhearted tries, and so
those who failed must lose their lives.

Many a young man tried, for 'tis well known
how easily a woman talks, and 'tis not unpleasant
to marry a princess and own half a kingdom.
But alas, these fine young men all failed, for the
princess could not be persuaded to say a word,
and one by one, they lost their lives.

Finally word of the stubborn girl reached the ears of the new page, and he decided to try his luck with her. Into her chamber he walked one morning, and without giving her so much as a glance, went up to her mirror.

"Good morning, little mirror," he said. "I want to tell you a story. But remember, 'tis only a story. Once upon a time three men went for a walk in the country. They were an artist, a tailor, and a teacher. Now, little mirror, when night came, they had to keep a fire burning to guard themselves from the wild animals, so it was decided that while two of them slept, the other one should tend the fire.

"It was the artist's turn first—but remember this is only a story, little mirror—and as his companions lay snoring, he looked about for something to keep him awake, and what should he find but a tiny baby hidden in the grass! Then the tailor awakened, and quick as a wink, he made a fine dress for the child. Then the teacher awakened, and in a trice he taught the baby to

54

speak. Now, little mirror—though you must remember this is only a story—to whom did the
baby belong, to the artist, or the tailor, or the
teacher? Think hard, little mirror, but remember this is only a story."

Then the princess cried out, "It belonged to
the artist, of course, for he found it." And she
danced up and down with excitement.

"That is right, very right," cried the lad, and
all aquiver with excitement himself, he ran out
the door to proclaim his success in making the
princess talk.

But alas, alack, where should he run but
straight into the arms of the king's hangmen,
and as they had neither seen nor heard the princess and would believe nothing but their own
eyes and ears, they called the lad's story a tall
tale, and hustled him out to the courtyard to be
hanged.

And dead as a herring the poor boy soon would
have been, but just at that moment Mistress
Good Luck and Dame Know-All came walking

by and discovered his plight.

"Well," cried Mistress Good Luck, "just see what wisdom and learning have done for this poor boy! He stands on the gallows before half his life is run, and nothing but good fortune can save him."

"Then give it to him, and be quick about it," cried Dame Know-All.

"Very well," said Mistress Good Luck. "But then will you still say that great knowledge is better than good fortune?"

No indeed, Dame Know-All would not, and so Mistress Good Luck waved the wand of fortune over the courtyard, and that brought the princess running from the palace and straight into the arms of the young lad.

"If you hang this boy, you will hang yourselves," she cried. "He told me a wonderful story and made me talk, and now I want to marry him if he will accept my hand."

Well, the hangmen wanted to keep their own heads, gray and bald though they were, and as it was plain to be seen that the princess was talking again, they let the lad go at once. Then the boy accepted the hand of the princess quite willingly, and soon they were married with great pomp and splendor.

And they lived happily ever after, happily indeed, for the lad's good luck never deserted him, and the princess always said just the right thing, never too much and never too little.

THE THREE TAILORS
AND THE WHITE
GOOSE

Once upon a time there were three young
tailors. They had clever fingers and sharp
scissors, but never a customer came to their doors,
and so one day they gave up tailoring and went

out into the wide world to seek their fortunes.

On their way, they came to a deep, dark forest, and here they lost their way and wandered round and round till it was black evening and they were sore and hungry. Then suddenly, in the distance, they saw a wonderful castle that shone like diamonds, and they turned and ran toward it. But at the gates, strange to tell, they saw no guards, and when they knocked at the palace door, there was no answer.

"Shall we enter?" said the first tailor.

"Let us, indeed," said the other two, and so in they went and stood in a great hall with a floor all jeweled and walls of gold. But still not a soul was to be seen, and so on they went from room to room until they reached the kitchen, and here they found a white goose sweeping and dusting the hearth.

"Greetings, my friends," said the white goose, coming forward and bending her neck, as a well-bred goose should always do, and the tailors, who were glad to find something alive even if it were

only a goose, answered, "Greetings we return, friend goose."

"You are just in time for a fine supper," said the goose, and she threw open the pantry door and showed them cupboards filled to bursting with a dozen good things to eat, cakes and tarts, and candies with caraway seeds.

"Thank you kindly," said the tailors, and while the goose made a fire in the stove, fanning it briskly with her wings to set the flames dancing, the tailors made a wonderful supper, and carrying it into the palace dining room—for it was much too fine a meal to eat in the kitchen—ate to their hearts' content.

When they had finished, they thanked the goose, and then she said, "You have eaten well, and now you shall sleep well, too," and she led them out of the dining room, down a long golden hall, and into a great bedroom where there stood three beds piled soft and high with silk and eider down.

"Good night and sleep tight," said the white

goose. "But be pleased to remember one thing. When the clock strikes twelve, a beautiful girl will enter the room, and she will offer you cakes and wine. But you must refuse to taste even so much as a crumb no matter how hungry or thirsty you feel. Do you promise to remember that?"

Yes, the men promised, and so she left, and the men went straight to bed and fell fast asleep. But as soon as the clock struck twelve, they were awakened, and through the door came the most beautiful girl they had ever seen, with hair like spun gold and eyes blue as the sea. And just as the white goose had predicted, the maiden offered them dainty cakes and glasses of shimmering wine.

But the men shook their heads. "No, thank you," they said. "We ate plenty, and more, at supper, and there isn't room for another crumb." And so the beautiful maiden had to leave with her cups of wine and her dainty cakes, and the three tailors went back to sleep and slept peace-

fully till the sun was high in the sky. Then they
got up and dressed and went to the kitchen where
the goose had breakfast waiting for them.

"I see you slept well," said the goose.

"Very well, and thank you kindly," said the
men.

"And you kept your promise, too," said the
goose. "And since you have done that I hope you
can break the spell under which this castle and
the forest lie."

"We will try," said the tailors, for they wished
to repay the kindness of the white goose.

"Somewhere in the forest dwells a witch," said
the goose. "Whether to north or south, or east
or west, I dare not say, but find her you can, if
you are but brave. One thing, however, you
must promise me."

"You have only to name it," said the tailors.

"On your way you will find a tree that bears
golden leaves from morn till midnight, but no
matter how the leaves glitter, you must not touch
them, for then you will never find the witch,

and the enchantment will be stronger than ever."

"That promise we will keep," said the tailors, and so they fell to eating a good breakfast, and then left the castle in search of the wicked witch.

They walked all morning through fine gardens and groves of lovely trees, and came at last to a garden more beautiful than all the rest, with flowers that sparkled like jewels, and trees that sang in the wind. And here, in the center of the garden, stood the tree that grew leaves of gold from morn till midnight. The leaves sparkled bright as the sun, and their music was the sound of golden chimes.

"What a sight," cried the first tailor. "Whoever owned but a pocketful of those leaves would be rich for the rest of his days."

"Well," said the second tailor, "why should we pass up such a golden opportunity? Who would wish to run in search of witches when he can take his weight in gold without the least danger?"

The first tailor agreed with his companion,

but the third tailor thought otherwise. "We promised the white goose that we would break the enchantment and not touch the tree with the golden leaves," he said, "and I will stand by that promise through thick and thin." And so while the others stuffed their pockets and shirts with golden leaves, and then turned back toward home again, he went deeper into the forest in search of the wicked witch.

Finally, far in the distance, he heard the sound of sweet music, and turning in that direction, he walked and walked until he came to a hill. At the top a great giant lay pegged to the ground with ropes, and over him trampled a flock of white geese, over and back, and up and down, while near by a beautiful young woman sat playing a harp—the same beautiful maiden who had offered cakes and wine to the tailors on the previous night.

The giant looked up at the tailor and cried, "If you have a heart in your body, kind sir, take the club that lies at my feet and strike me dead, for 'tis better to die quickly than to be trampled slowly to death by all these geese."

Now, 'twas little enough the tailor liked striking the giant, but as this was the poor fellow's wish, he took up the club at once and struck him a mighty blow square on the forehead. Then there was a great trembling in the earth and all the geese were changed into footmen and maidservants, while the giant and the white goose from the castle turned into a handsome prince and a beautiful princess. But the maiden with the harp was changed into a witch, and away she flew, never to be seen again.

"We thank you for your bravery," said the prince and the princess. "And now we will reward you quite suitably. Here is a magic tablecloth, and with it you will never want for food or drink. All you need do when you are hungry is spread out the cloth and say, 'Cloth, serve me quickly, cloth, serve me well,' and you will have all you can eat, and more, too."

"I thank you kindly," said the tailor, accepting the cloth, and then he bid his friends good-bye and started for home.

When he reached the open country beyond the forest, he grew hungry, so he spread the magic cloth on the grass and said, "Cloth, serve me quickly, cloth, serve me well," and there in a moment were good things enough to feed the tailor twice over, roast ham, and white bread and butter, and plenty of sweets and jelly tarts.

The tailor ate to bursting and then lay down to rest, but scarcely had he settled himself when up rode two great giants.

"Ah!" cried the giants. "So you've eaten without us and saved nothing for us! Well, little man, you'd best hurry another fine meal for us else you'll be served up as hash yourself."

Now the tailor hardly wished to disclose the secret of his magic cloth, but much less did he wish to be hash for the giants, so he said, "Cloth, serve me quickly, cloth, serve me well," and all at once the cloth was covered with a huge and splendid banquet.

Then the giants fell to eating and seemed quite pleased with the little tailor and thanked him for his generosity. But all the time they had their eyes on the cloth, and when they had finished, they said, " 'Tis a fine cloth you have here. For what will you sell it?"

"There is not gold enough in the whole kingdom to pay for this cloth," said the tailor.

"We will trade it to you for a magic sack we have here," said the giants. "When you open it and call, 'Everyone out,' you will have a whole army of soldiers at your command, and they will do whatever you wish until you cry, 'Everyone in.' "

"No, thank you," said the tailor. "What could I do with soldiers but fight a war? I would rather eat well than kill people."

Then the giants roared, "Take the sack or not, as you choose, but we will have the cloth!" And with that, they threw the sack at the tailor, knocked the poor fellow over, and then snatched the cloth, and were off and out of sight in a minute.

The tailor rose from the ground and said to himself, "Well, I do not care to be pushed about, especially by giants, so I shall teach them a lesson or two," and he picked up the sack, opened it, and said, "Everyone out." Then out like the rush of a great wind came soldier after soldier till there was a regular army of them.

"Now," said the tailor, "two giants have stolen my tablecloth, and you must pursue them and capture it."

"As you bid," said the captain of the soldiers, and away they went in pursuit of the giants. They soon caught up with them, but as one giant was almost as big as a whole regiment of soldiers and could toss bullets back like rubber balls, the battle for the cloth was long and fierce. But at last the giants were defeated, and with the precious cloth safe in their hands, the soldiers marched back to the tailor.

"You have served me well," said the tailor. "Now everyone in," and into the sack all the soldiers disappeared.

Then the tailor journeyed on toward home, and as he neared the town, looking dusty and tired from his long trip, whom should he meet but his two tailor friends, rich merchants now, and dressed with pomp and splendor.

"Greetings to you, my friends," said the weary traveler.

"Ah, 'tis the poor tailor," exclaimed the two rich men, looking down their noses. "Well, did you free the enchanted forest, and earn something for your pains?"

"I earned enough," said the tailor.

"But not so much as we," said his former companions.

"Then perhaps you will help me," said the tailor.

But oh dear, no, the rich men could not help him. After all, had he wished, he too could have taken the golden leaves that shimmered like the sun in that faraway garden of enchantment. But no, he must seek the witch and get little for his trouble.

"Very well," said the tailor. "If you will not help me, 'tis so, and there's little use to cry about it. But perhaps, for old time's sake, you will come and dine with me, and though we'll not eat like kings, we'll break the sweet bread of friendship."

And to this the rich men agreed, for of course, it took nothing out of their pockets, and the next day, dressed in their second best satin suits and driving their second best carriages, they came to the tailor's house. The good man greeted them, and then spreading the white cloth on the table before them said, "Cloth, serve me quickly, cloth, serve me well," and there in an instant was a feast fit for a king.

"Where did you get this wonderful cloth?" exclaimed the guests.

"Oh, 'twas a gift from the white goose," said the tailor. "And 'twill always serve me food and drink aplenty."

At this the rich men were so filled with envy

they could scarcely eat a mouthful of the wonderful banquet, and when the tailor left the room for a moment, the first man said, "We must steal this cloth from that stupid little tailor and go far away where he will never find us. We might easily use up all our gold, but we could never be poor with a cloth like this."

"How very true," said the second man. "Yes indeed, we must make away with the cloth." And so that night when the tailor lay fast asleep, they returned to the house, took the treasure, and made off for a far country.

In the morning, however, the tailor soon discovered his loss, and then he opened his trusty sack and called, "Everyone out," and out like a rush of wind poured the soldiers till there was a whole regiment of them.

"Go after those rich men who stole my cloth!" cried the tailor, and away rushed the soldiers. And as the rich men were no giants, the soldiers soon rescued the cloth, and gave the rascals such a scare they never dared to come back. Then the soldiers returned with the cloth, and the tailor said, "You have served me well, and now everyone in," and back into the bag went all the soldiers.

From that time on, the tailor had no further trouble, but instead won fame and fortune, for his cloth served such wonderful meals that soon no one in the kingdom was ever hungry, and his sackful of soldiers fought and won all the wars. The king made him a general and master of the palace kitchen, and the whole kingdom lived happily ever after.

THE SUITOR

THERE was once a handsome young fellow named Tom who had inherited a fine farm from a rich old uncle, and now decided it was time to find himself a wife. But not an ordinary wife, indeed not, for what with the farm and one thing and another, Tom considered himself quite wealthy, and as we all know, the wives of wealthy men must always be prettier and wiser than those of the poor.

Tom wanted a wife who was beautiful and industrious, wise and good, and of course, it would do no harm if she possessed some property. So one day he rode over to the home of a rich farmer who lived in the neighborhood and had three daughters, each ready to be married at once. Tom had never spoken to the daughters, but he had seen them from afar, and he was sure that one of them would make a good wife.

These girls, however, had one great fault. They did not speak distinctly, and when Tom came to call on them, they were sent to their spinning and forbidden to say a word. Their father greeted the lad, and their mother fed him well, but the girls had to stay in a corner and keep silently at their work.

All of a sudden, however, one of them broke her thread, and she quickly forgot that she had been forbidden to speak. "My thwead!" she cried. "My thwead, it bwoke!"

"Tie it adain," exclaimed the second sister, and the third one added, "Mamma told us not to talk, and now we tan't teep still."

When Tom heard these grown girls talking like babies, he was quite angry, and he hurried away at once, for he little wanted a wife who could not speak distinctly.

A few days later he went on to another farm where there lived a young lady who was considered exceedingly fine in every way, and whom he was anxious to meet. But, alas, she had her failings, too. She talked like a house afire, and her spinning wheel went just as fast.

"How long does it take you to use up a large head of flax?" the young man asked her.

"Only a few hours," answered the girl airily.

Then she left the room for a moment to look after the servants, and Tom seized a key from a near-by bureau and stuffed it into the head of flax with which she had just been spinning. When the girl came back, he did not mention the key, but went on talking as if nothing had happened, and when it was time to go, he said good-bye and promised to call again in a week.

Next week to the day, Tom returned, and when he came into the room, there sat the young lady as busy as ever with her spinning. But strange to say, she was dressed in her poorest clothes, and when she had bidden Tom sit down, she told him a surprising tale.

"The key to my bureau is missing," she said. "And though we have looked in the house and out the house, we cannot find it anywhere, and I don't know what I shall do, for all my fine things are locked up!"

"How sad indeed that the key is missing!" exclaimed Tom. Then without another word, he walked over to the ball of flax and pulled out the key from the very spot where he had hidden it a week ago. Then he bid the girl good-bye, and hurried on his way, for he wanted none of a woman who talked faster than she worked, and stretched the truth besides.

Sometime later, Tom heard of a girl who was

not only pretty and clever, but also wise and good. She had fine parents, too, people said, so the lad saddled his horse and rode over to have a look at her.

Everyone was at home, and Tom was received very kindly. While he talked with the father about the weather and the crops, the girl and her mother prepared the finest meal that the house could offer.

When all was ready, the mother said to the girl, "Go into the cellar and fetch a bottle of wine." This the girl started to do, but once in the cellar, she got to thinking of her wedding gown, and wondered so hard about what pattern she would choose, that she sat down on a stool, thought more and more, and forgot the wine entirely.

While she was gone, the parents told Tom of their daughter's many fine qualities, what a good worker she was, how kind, how clever, and so on and so forth, until Tom said to himself, "I do believe she is just the wife I want," and he began to wait excitedly for her return. But she did not come back, and presently her mother went to see what had become of her.

When she found her sitting dreamily in the cellar, she exclaimed, "What is the matter, daughter? Why didn't you bring up the wine?"

"Well, Mother," said the daughter, "I am thinking that if I marry Tom, I must be very careful about the pattern that I choose for my wedding gown. The question is, what pattern would be best?"

"Now there's a question that is a question," answered the mother. "Yes indeed, what pattern will be best?" And she herself sat down by her daughter to think over this important matter.

Upstairs, the farmer and Tom waited and waited, but neither the wife nor the daughter came back. Finally the farmer exclaimed a little angrily, "Now what can be keeping that wife and daughter of mine? I shall have to go and fetch both of them."

So he, too, went into the cellar, and there he

found his family sitting and saying never a word. "What are you doing here?" he cried. "You have kept us waiting for over an hour!"

"We are thinking," said his wife.

"Thinking!" cried the farmer. "And why should you think?"

"If our daughter is to marry Tom," said the wife, "she must have a fine gown, but to make a fine gown, we must have the right pattern, and that is a matter requiring deep thought."

The former nodded. He saw things in a different light now. "You are indeed right, my good wife," he said, and then he, too, sat down to consider the matter.

Now Tom had to wait by himself, but as this grew tiresome, he also went to the cellar to see what had happened. There he found them all sitting and saying never a word, and he cried, "What is the meaning of this? Why do you sit here and leave me alone upstairs?"

There was no answer at first. But after a time, the farmer roused from his reverie and explained their problem.

"We are thinking about the pattern for our daughter's wedding dress," he said. "If she is to marry a rich lad like you, she must have a fine gown, and the pattern is most important."

"Indeed it is," answered Tom. "What *will* be the best pattern? Well, you may think about it until I return, and in the meantime, I will do the same." Then he bid them good-bye, and mounting his horse, rode home as fast as he could.

And if he has not found a girl who does very little thinking, he is still a bachelor. As to the farmer and his wife and daughter, they may yet, for all I know, be sitting in that cellar, thinking and thinking of a pattern for the wedding gown!

THE WONDERFUL
KNAPSACK

ONCE upon a time there was a soldier
who had served his king well for ten
years and a day, but alas, alack, when he came
to get his pay for all the wars he had won, the
king was as poor as he, and there were only
three pennies left in the royal treasury.

"Well," said the soldier, "I'll not worry about it. I'll take my pay in honor and glory."

"To be sure," said the king, "honor and glory are all very well, but they'll not keep the wolf from the door. I will give you the palace plates. They are pure gold and will sell for a high price."

"Then you could not eat like a king," cried the soldier, "and that would never do. No indeed, your majesty, give me the three pennies and I will be on my way."

"Very well then," said the king, and he scooped up the three lone pennies from the bottom of the royal treasury and laid them in the hand of the soldier. "May they bring you luck," he said, and the soldier thanked him and went whistling on his way.

Now, when he had walked a mile or so, whom should he meet but an old, old crone, bent in the middle and with scarcely a tooth in her head.

"A penny from the young for the old," begged the old woman.

"A penny!" exclaimed the soldier. "Why,

I've but three pennies in the whole, wide world. Still, it little matters if there are three or two," and so he gave the old woman one of the pennies.

Then he walked on another mile or so, till what should he come upon but a second old crone more bent and toothless than the first!

"A penny from the young for the old," begged the old woman.

"A penny!" cried the soldier. "Why, all I have in the whole, wide world is two pennies. Still, it little matters if there's two or one," and he gave the old woman the second of the pennies.

Then he walked on with the one lone penny, till after a mile or so he was stopped by a third old crone so bent that her chin almost touched her knees.

"A penny from the young for the old," said this old creature, and the soldier exclaimed, "One penny is all I have in the world. But it little matters if I've one or none," and he gave the last penny to the old woman.

At this, the old creature changed into a young

and beautiful girl, for she was not really an old crone at all, but a fairy who had tested the soldier three times to see if he were good and brave.

"What a kind and generous lad you are," exclaimed the fairy. "And for that you deserve to be generously rewarded. I will give you three wishes, and all of them will come true."

But what do you know, the soldier could not think of a thing to wish for! He had two strong arms, two long legs, and a head set straight on his shoulders, and that was all he had ever wanted. At length, however, he said, "I wish to have a long life and a healthy one."

"You have wished a good wish," said the fairy. "Now for your other wishes."

Now the soldier had a knapsack that had been with him in the wars, and he liked the fit and the feel of it, particularly when it was full, so at last he said, "I wish that my knapsack will never wear out. And I wish last, that whatever I want will go into my knapsack, and whatever

I want will come out."

"Three better wishes were never made," said the fairy, "nor three more easily granted. Now good-bye, and good luck." And with that the fairy disappeared, and the soldier went happily on his way.

Toward evening he reached the town, and as he was very hungry, in he walked to the best inn and sat down at the finest table. "Landlord," he called, "serve me food, and serve it well," and the landlord came running.

But when the landlord saw a torn and tattered soldier instead of a silk and satin lord, he cried, "We will feed you food aplenty, good soldier, but you must come into the kitchen."

"No, thank you," said the soldier. "This will do quite nicely, I am sure. Of course, I am used to finer linen and brighter candlelight, but as I am hungry, it will not matter. Now bring me two bottles of your best wine and a dozen chicken breasts and be quick about it."

At this bold talk, the landlord quickly

changed his tune, for of course, no plain, ordinary soldier would speak in such a fashion, and this one must surely be a prince in disguise.

"Yes, sir, whatever you wish, sir," he said politely, and then he ran to set the table with his finest linen and dishes and to serve the food just as the soldier had ordered.

When all was ready, the soldier fell to eating at once, for he was quite famished, but near the end, he remembered to leave a good bit on his plate, since that, of course, is always what lords and ladies do. Then he wished a handful of gold coins into the knapsack, and taking out two of them, tossed them to the landlord.

"I trust this will pay for the meal," he said.

"It is payment, and more," said the landlord, and he bowed so low he bumped his head on the floor. "I hope everything suited your taste, your excellency."

"Fairly well, my good man," said the soldier. "Now you must provide me with a room for the night."

But alas, there were no rooms—and the land-lord almost wept to say this—there were no rooms save one, and that could not be used.

"And why not?" exclaimed the soldier.

"Who goes in there alive comes out dead," cried the landlord.

"Is that all?" laughed the soldier. "Then that is the very room for me. Sweep it clean and make the bed well, for I am tired tonight."

The landlord wrung his hands, and the maids cried, and all the rich diners shook their heads, but nothing would do but that the soldier sleep in the dreadful room; and so it was prepared, and when the soldier had smoked awhile by the fire and felt a little drowsy, he bid everyone good night and went up to it.

Inside, he locked the door, stood his faithful knapsack in a corner where he could keep his eye on it, and sat down in a chair to see what would happen.

He had only a moment to wait until there was a great rustling in the chimney and a black ball came rolling out of the fireplace and into the center of the room. There it unrolled itself, and the soldier saw the ugliest troll ever seen in the whole, wide world, with eyes red as fire and fingers like claws. Then out rolled a second troll, and after that a third, each uglier than the other, and both much worse than the first.

"How do you do?" said the soldier. "How very nice of you to come and keep me company! Now do sit down and make yourselves at home," and he pointed to three chairs on the other side of the fireplace.

The three trolls seated themselves, but not for long. In a minute they were up and at the soldier. One tweaked his nose, the other pulled his ears, and the third one tried to pin down his arms.

"Dear me," said the soldier, "I must say this is a strange way for guests to act. Well, if you can do no better, into my knapsack you must go." And there and then, into the knapsack they had to creep, and soon only a creaking and hissing could be heard.

"I hope you are comfortable there," said the soldier. "But if you are not, 'tis your own fault, to be sure. And now you must answer me a question. Why do you pester this room every night?"

There was a great silence for a moment, but whether they would or nay, the trolls had to give up their secret.

"We guard the oven," said the first.

"To protect a treasure," said the second.

"And woe to him who tries to steal it," said the third.

"Very well," said the soldier. "And thank you for your information." Then he undressed, for he was very tired, and went straight to bed.

Next morning the landlord, and the maids, and all the rich diners came to see what had happened to the remarkable soldier. They knocked on the door and peeked through the keyhole, but as the soldier was still sleeping he did not hear them, and so they thought he was dead and set up a great weeping and wailing.

"He was so young and handsome," cried all the maids.

"He was so rich," cried the landlord.

"And he ate like a prince," cried all the rich diners.

Now all this fuss and bother finally awakened the soldier, and he cried out crossly, "Landlord, landlord, what's all this fuss?"

"Oh, my!" cried everyone. "You're not still alive, are you?"

"Alive and ready to eat," answered the soldier. "Landlord, serve me a dozen fresh eggs and a pail of warm milk."

This the landlord ran to do, followed by the maids and diners, and when all was ready, the soldier got up and dressed, took a good look at his knapsack, then locked his room and went down to eat.

And when he had eaten, he commanded the landlord to bring him three strong men. "They must take my knapsack to the blacksmith's and beat the dust out of it," said the soldier. "I have walked a long mile or two in my day, and the knapsack is powerfully dusty."

The landlord did as he was ordered, though truth to tell, he considered it quite a strange request, and soon three strong men were lugging and tugging at the knapsack which looked light as a feather but weighed heavy as lead. And when they reached the blacksmith's shop, they were so tired they could hardly lift a finger, to say nothing of wielding a heavy hammer, so three of the blacksmith's strongest helpers were set to the task of beating the knapsack.

But what a shrieking was heard when they started their work, shrieking enough to set your hair on end!

"Don't mind a little noise," said the soldier. "My knapsack is squeaky at the seams. Just beat as hard as you can."

So the men went on, and after a while, all was quiet. Then the soldier said, "There, that's clean enough. Now be so good as to empty it into the sea."

But these poor fellows were now so tired they could scarce lift a finger, to say nothing of carrying a heavy knapsack down to the sea, so three more huskies were found, and they lugged and tugged till the strange knapsack was down to the shore. Then they opened it, and what a pile of black dust poured into the water! It was all that was left of the three dreadful trolls, and good riddance, too, though it blackened the sea for a mile around.

The workmen were now paid for their hard labor, and generously, too, with a handful of gold for each of them, and then the soldier returned to the landlord.

"Landlord," he cried, "I have one last task for you. In the room where I slept last night, there stands a big oven, and this you must tear down at once."

"Well," said the landlord to himself, "he'll soon want to pull down the roof from over my head, but I'll not question money." So he did as the soldier commanded, and there under the

THE WONDERFUL KNAPSACK

oven, what should he find but a pot of gold as big as a washtub!

"What a clever fellow you were to discover all this gold," exclaimed the landlord.

"Oh, 'twas nothing at all," said the soldier. "Now take it, good landlord, all of it, and use it well." Then he took up his knapsack and bid his host good-bye. But the landlord would not let him go without half the money, and this he could not refuse. But it was a heavy load to carry, and so he must stay a bit longer. And then whom should he meet but the landlord's daughter, a very pretty lass, and so he must tarry still longer, till the lass was his bride, and then— well, with health, wealth, and happiness, he no doubt tarries there still.

DOCTOR AND
DETECTIVE, TOO

ONCE an old farmer was driving to town
with a load of turf which he hoped to sell
for a good price. On the way he chanced to
meet a doctor. This worthy man walked along
in a fine manner, wearing a cape and tall doctor's
hat, with a cane and doctor book under his arm,
and in his mouth a long, long pipe.

The farmer tipped his hat respectfully, and the doctor said, "Good day, my good man. I would like to buy your turf."

"And I would like to sell it," said the farmer. "But you must pay me well."

"I will give you my fine cloak," said the doctor.

But this was not enough, and so they argued this way and that, until the doctor had to offer not only his cloak, but his tall hat as well, and also his long pipe, and his fine cane and doctor book. Then the farmer was satisfied and the bargain was closed. The doctor rode off with the load of turf, and the farmer walked home with the doctor's clothes.

It was late when he arrived, and his wife was anxiously waiting for him. "I hope you made a good bargain," she said.

"Better than good," said the farmer, and he displayed his doctor's clothes.

But his wife did not find it better than good. "How can we get bread and butter with such rubbish?" she cried. "You should have sold the turf for money."

"We shall have money and more," said her husband, "for I have decided to be a doctor myself. I have a doctor's cloak and cap, and pray, what more do I need?"

Then he put on the mantle and hat, and with the long pipe in his mouth, he sat from morning till night reading and reading in the large doctor book. He looked exactly like a real doctor and no one would have noticed the slightest difference. But still he made no money, for never a patient came to see him.

Finally, he said to himself, "I daresay people would flock to me if they knew who I was. I will put up a sign declaring that here lives the greatest doctor in the world." And then and there he sat down and painted a sign. But as he knew very little about writing—in fact this was the first time he had ever tried it—he wrote: "Here lives the Greatest Detective in the world," and never knew the difference.

A few days later, the king happened to pass the farmer's house, and he saw the sign and said, "I will remember that the greatest detective in the world lives here, and someday I will make use of him."

And make use of him, he did, for not two days later, a thief entered the royal stables and stole two of the king's best horses. The king was very angry and sent his guards to search everywhere for the lost animals. But they could not be found, though the guards searched a week and a day, and looked from one end of the country to the other.

Then the king remembered the famous detective. "Now we shall find our horses and solve this mystery," he cried, and he sent one of his guards back at top speed to get help from this wise man.

The guard arrived in no time at all, and he found the farmer seated as usual, with the big doctor book propped up in front of him. He took off his hat, then bowed politely and started to speak, but before he had said more than a word, the farmer stopped him. "You need tell me nothing," said the farmer. "I know everything already."

"You are truly a great detective," exclaimed the messenger. "Will you kindly tell me where to find them?"

"Yes indeed," replied the farmer, and he looked very wise and slowly turned the pages of the doctor book. Then he took out a slip of paper which he had found in the book, and folded it, and handed it to the messenger. "Go to the druggist and get this medicine," he said, and he sounded like a real doctor. "Take it at once, and you will be sure to find them."

The messenger lost no time in getting the medicine, and as soon as it was in his hands, he took a big dose of it. Then he set out at a lively pace toward the palace, for he was anxious to tell the king about the amazing detective who knew everything.

He had not gone far, however, before the

medicine began to make him feel very ill, and he had to stop at a farmhouse and ask for help. The farmer's wife took him in and bade him lie down on her best couch. But the poor fellow felt worse than ever—in fact, he thought he was going to die. Just as he was sure he had drawn his last breath, however, he heard a familiar neighing from the stable across the courtyard. This made him forget all about dying, and he leaped up and ran to the window. And there, sure enough, he saw the king's horses prancing, and neighing, and glittering in the sunlight; and jumping out the window, and running to the stable, he quickly caught them and raced back to the palace.

When the king saw his lost treasures, he was overjoyed and hardly knew how to praise and reward the great detective. But as a small token of his esteem and gratitude, he sent him a large bag of money. When the farmer received the money, he said to his wife, "Well, my good woman, a doctor's trade is indeed an easy one.

Now did I not do better than good when I traded my turf for some doctor's clothes?"

"Indeed yes," exclaimed his wife, and she made off with half the money to buy herself some fine new clothes.

Sometime later, a beautiful gold ring belonging to the king's daughter was stolen, and though the guards searched everywhere, from the north to the south, they could find no trace of it. Then the king remembered the great detective. "There is the very man to solve this difficult affair," he said, and he lost no time in dispatching a messenger to invite the famous man to the palace.

When the messenger arrived, there sat the farmer looking very wise, with his pipe in his mouth and his book under his nose. And when the messenger opened his mouth to speak, the farmer said, "You need tell me nothing. I know it all, and I am willing to come." Then he put on his fine cloak and hat, and with his wife and cane on one arm, and his doctor book under the other, he entered the royal coach and was driven back to the palace.

When he arrived, who should open the door but the king himself, and his royal highness bowed so low before his company that he almost lost his crown. Then he invited the farmer and his wife to a state dinner. "We will eat roast goose, and strawberry tarts, and a dozen other good things, all on the queen's best gold plates," he said. "And tomorrow, if you are willing, we will search for the ring."

The farmer was willing, and the king led them into the palace dining room. And there, indeed, was a sight to blind your eyes, if you weren't used to palace life. The table was set from end to end with gold, and silver, and dazzling crystal.

"This *will* be a banquet!" the farmer exclaimed to his wife. "We must be sure to count all the dishes they serve. There will be more than a dozen, I know. There will be a hundred or more."

The wife nodded, and then they were seated, and the door opened and in came a servant with the first dish. The farmer looked at his wife and said, "This is the first one," and then busied himself with eating the wonderful dish.

Meanwhile, the servant, who had overheard the farmer's words, turned pale as a ghost. He thought the great detective had meant "Here is the first thief," and as he really was a thief and with two other servants had stolen the princess's ring, he was now sure that the crime had been discovered.

Pale and trembling with fright, the guilty servant ran back to his friends in the kitchen and exclaimed, "The great detective sits at the dinner table and knows I am the first thief! We must do something to save ourselves!"

But just then it was time for the second servant to carry in the next dish. "Ask the great man to step into the kitchen," cried the other two servants. "Then perhaps we can beg for mercy and he will spare our lives."

The servant went into the dining hall, and as he set down his dish, the farmer said to his wife, "This is the second one."

The wife nodded, and the servant grew pale as a sheet, and pulled at the farmer's sleeve to get his attention. But that good man was too interested in the fine food to notice the servant's distress, and so he had to return to the kitchen as helpless as his companion.

Now it was the third servant's turn. And when he brought in his dish, and the farmer said, "This is the third one," he pulled the farmer's sleeve so hard that it was almost torn, and he had to turn round.

"Great, wise sir," whispered the servant in a trembling voice, "will you come with me into the kitchen?"

The good farmer was completely surprised by these words, but since he was a very obliging fellow, he said, "I will come, and gladly," and he got up and followed the trembling servant into the kitchen.

Here the three servants cried, "Spare us, spare us! We did steal the ring, but you must spare us."

All was now clear to the farmer, so he scowled at the culprits and said in a stern voice, "You are great rascals and deserve severe punishment. I am afraid you will all have to be hung."

The servants fell on their knees. "Please show us mercy," cried the first.

"We will give back the ring if you will keep our secret," said the second.

"And we will give you two hundred dollars," cried the third.

"Very well," said the farmer. "I will keep your secret, but you must do just as I tell you. You must bake a cake with the ring inside and serve it to the king first thing tomorrow."

This the thieves promised to do, and the next morning at breakfast, the king had the finest cake he had ever seen set before him. And while they ate their first course, the king said to the farmer, "It is high time we searched for the ring.

What help can you give me?"

"You need worry no longer," said the farmer. "The ring is here in this room."

"In this room!" cried the king, looking round in amazement.

The farmer nodded wisely. "Cut into the cake," he said, "and you shall see what you shall see."

The king cut into the cake, and there in the center, sure enough, lay the shining gold ring.

"You are the most remarkable man in the world!" cried the king to the farmer, and thereupon he gave him a bucketful of gold, and so too did the princess, and the three servants paid him the two hundred dollars which they owed him for keeping their secret. All in all, it was a good bit of money, and considerably more than anyone but you and I would know what to do with.

And from that day on, the farmer was so famous as a great detective that no one in the kingdom ever dared steal again. All the locksmiths went out of business, for people no longer needed locks and keys, and the king and the farmer and everyone else lived happily ever after.

PETER HUMBUG AND
THE WHITE CAT

IN a faraway country, there once lived a great
and powerful king who had three sons. The
two older boys were very handsome and clever,
but the youngest was considered of little account.
Peter was his name, and his brothers, calling

him Peter Humbug, made fun of him whenever they could. The king, however, loved them all equally well, and when he grew old, he could not decide which of them should have the throne.

Now in those days, it was the custom to keep the palace guarded with a heavy iron chain, so that the common people could not run in and out. The present chain needed replacing, however, and so the king, who was a very practical man and always enjoyed killing two birds at one shot, hit upon a clever scheme that would provide him with a new chain and solve the problem of his successor, both at the same time.

Calling his sons to him, the king explained his plan. "You must all set out to find a new chain for the palace," he said. "A year from today you will return, and the one who has the longest chain will succeed me to the throne."

The two older boys at once departed. The one found work with the finest blacksmith in the country, while the other went to work for the country's finest coppersmith.

As for Peter, he did not know where to go. But being a good son, he started out, taking the first path that he came to. This led through the countryside and into a forest, and here, alas, he lost his way. But as night fell, he saw a light shining in the distance, and walking toward it, he came to a small house. He knocked on the door, someone called, "Come in," and he opened the door and entered.

And inside, what should he find but a big white cat seated comfortably in a chair by the window! A big white cat and nothing more! He was so surprised he hardly knew what to do, but since he was a well-brought-up young man, he finally managed to say politely, "I am very tired. May I please rest here tonight?"

The cat nodded. "You are quite welcome," she said. "And since you come so late, you are no doubt hungry as well as tired."

"There is truth in those words," said Peter, and with that, the cat gave him a fine meal in the pantry and a fine bed in the corner. He ate heartily, then went to bed, and was soon fast asleep.

The next morning the cat said, "What is your name, young man, and where are you going?"

"I have been sent to find a chain long enough to go round my father's palace," answered Peter. "But I do not know where to find one or how to make it, and I have given up all hope of winning my father's kingdom."

"Well then, you can stay here and serve me if you wish," said the cat. "You will receive no wages, and the meals will be exactly like the one you had last night. But you will have nothing to do except wash and comb my fur three times a day."

"I could not find an easier task," said Peter, and so he stayed with the white cat for the year, washing and combing her three times each day, and spending the rest of his time in the woods.

When the year had passed, the cat said, "Now you must return home, Peter, so as to be there with your brothers."

But Peter did not want to go for he had no chain to take with him.

"Never fear," said the cat. "You shall have your chain. Just carry home the chest which you see standing in the hall, and after your brothers have shown their chains, you may open the chest, and there you will find a chain much longer and finer than either of the others."

"Thank you," said Peter. "I will do as you bid." Then he took the chest, said good-bye to the white cat, and left the little house in the forest.

When he reached home, his brothers had already arrived. "Let me see your chain," said the king to the oldest son.

The young man opened a strong chest and pulled out a heavy iron chain, which the king examined carefully. It reached once around the palace and was very strong. Then the second son displayed his masterpiece, the copper chain, and this reached twice around the palace.

And now it was Peter's turn. "Let us see what

my youngest son has brought," said the king, and Peter opened his chest and drew out a great chain which was neither iron nor copper, but pure gold that shone like the sun and reached three times around the palace.

At sight of this marvelous chain, everyone was amazed, and all agreed that Peter had done better than his brothers and should therefore inherit the kingdom. But the brothers themselves were not satisfied. They had been sure of winning the throne, and they considered Peter Humbug a poor fellow to manage a kingdom. So they gave the matter much thought, and at length they asked the king to send them away on another search. This time they were to look for money, and the one who returned with the largest amount would possess the throne.

The older brothers were sure they would win this time, for it takes a clever man to make a good deal of money, and Peter, you must remember, was considered of little account.

The first brother became a merchant and sold

his goods for many times what they were worth, while the second one became a money lender and lent gold at a fearful rate of interest.

As for Peter, he did not know what to do. But he started out again, and as his path took him through the countryside and into the forest, he presently reached the little house where he had stopped before. The white cat still lived here, and once again, at his entreaty, she gave him a fine dinner to eat and a soft bed in which to sleep.

And in the morning the cat said, "Will you stay with me another year, Peter? You will receive no wages, and the meals will be exactly like the one you had last night, but you will have nothing to do except wash and comb my fur three times a day."

"I will be glad to stay," said Peter, and during the whole year, he washed and combed the cat three times a day, and spent the other hours roaming through the woods.

The year went quickly by, and when the time

was up, the cat said to the young prince, "Now you must return home, Peter. Your brothers will soon be there."

"But I have no money," Peter objected.

"Take the chest that is in the hall," said the cat. "You will find money enough in that."

"Thank you kindly," said Peter. "I will do as you say." Then he took up the chest, and bidding the cat good-bye, was once again on his way.

The king and his brothers were waiting for him when he arrived at the palace, and as soon as he entered the door, the king said, "Now we shall see who has collected the most money. Open your chests, my sons." And the two older boys fell to unlocking their treasures at once. The first one had collected copper coins, and there were so many of them that they covered half the floor of the largest room in the palace.

The second son's treasure was of silver, and he had coins enough to cover the rest of the floor.

Then came Peter's turn. "Well, Peter Humbug," cried the brothers, "can you do better than we have done?"

"Perhaps not," said Peter, and the second son with all his silver began to see himself as the new king. Soon, however, Peter had opened his chest and emptied his money upon the floor. He spread it over the other coins, and when he had finished, not one copper or silver piece could be seen, for the whole floor glittered and sparkled with gold, Peter Humbug's gold.

"Peter is again the victor," declared the king. "And now there is no doubt that he will inherit the throne."

But still the brothers were not satisfied. "Peter is not clever enough to rule a kingdom," they cried, and they put their heads together, and then proposed a third and final test. This time their father should send them out to seek a wife, and the one who returned at the end of the year with the prettiest bride should win the throne.

The king was not altogether pleased with this

proposal, especially for Peter's sake, but as the young prince made no objection, he finally consented.

The brothers were now overjoyed, for they were sure that Peter could not possibly win this time. There was not one princess in the whole, wide world, not even an ugly one, who would willingly marry stupid Peter Humbug.

And Peter agreed with his brothers, and had his father not said, "Go at once, Peter, and luck be with you," he would have remained at home while his brothers searched for their beautiful brides.

But he was a dutiful son, so he obeyed his father, and setting out again, made his way through the countryside and into the forest. And after a time, what should he find but that same little hut where the white cat lived! He knocked at the door, the cat called, "Come in," and in he walked.

"I am very tired," said Peter. "May I rest here tonight?"

"With pleasure, my friend," said the cat. "And since you come so late, you are no doubt hungry as well as tired."

"That is not untrue," said Peter, and the cat gave him a fine meal in the pantry and a fine bed in the corner. He ate heartily, then went to bed and was soon fast asleep.

In the morning the cat said to him, "Why are you here again, Peter?"

"I have been sent to seek a wife," said Peter. "But, alas, I shall never find one."

"You had better stay with me then, Peter," said the cat. "You will receive no wages, and the meals will be the same as you had last night, but you will have nothing more to do than wash and comb my fur three times a day."

Now Peter was not sure that he should follow the cat's advice this time, for he must find a princess of great beauty in order to compete with his brothers, and hereabouts, he had not seen so much as a common servant girl. But as the cat had helped him so well before, he decided to stay.

Three times each day he washed and combed the cat, and the rest of the time he roamed through the woods. Thus the year went by, and when it was ended, the cat said to the young prince, "You must go home now, for both your brothers will soon be there, and each has a beautiful bride."

"But how can I go home?" cried Peter. "I have no bride for myself."

"Never fear," said the cat. "You have served me faithfully for three years, and now I will serve you. But you must promise to do exactly as I tell you."

Yes, Peter was ready to do whatever she wished!

"Now take your knife," continued the cat, "and cut off my head and strip off my skin."

"Oh, no," cried Peter. "I cannot do that. You have always treated me so kindly."

"But you must do it if you wish to find yourself a bride," replied the cat.

And so Peter had to obey. But no sooner had he cut off the cat's head than she changed into a princess, the most beautiful princess Peter had ever seen, with long golden hair, and a crown on her head.

What a surprise this was, and what a bigger surprise to hear the princess say, "Dear prince, you have freed me from an evil spell, and now, if you wish, I will return home with you and be your bride." Such a surprise it was that Peter could not say a word.

But he was able to nod his head and offer the princess his hand. Then she led him out of the house and into a golden carriage that stood conveniently waiting for them, and as they drove towards the palace, she told him all about herself and her strange life in the forest.

Her father had once been a great and powerful king, and had lived happily with his queen and their little daughter until the queen fell ill one day and died. Then the king married a wicked woman who had one ugly daughter, and when the new queen saw how pretty the little princess was, she grew so angry that she changed her into a white cat, and a white cat she had to stay until there came a prince who would willingly serve her three long years.

Peter had been that prince, and the princess, looking up at him, smiled so sweetly that he stopped the horses in the middle of the forest and kissed her.

A short time later, the young couple reached the palace. On the front steps stood the old king with his two sons and their wives. They had seen the carriage from afar and were wondering who could afford to ride in such luxury. When they saw it was Peter, their eyes almost fell out of their heads. And when Peter stepped from the carriage, and then helped the princess to alight, and they all saw how beautiful she was, they nearly jumped out of their skins. The two other princesses were very pretty girls, but they could not compare with Peter's fair and graceful bride.

It was thus decided that Peter should inherit

the throne, and this he did, shortly afterwards, when the old king had died, and his marriage to the princess had been celebrated with great splendor. And evidently he was a much better man than his brothers expected, for he ruled his land wisely and well, and was loved by all his subjects.

And what of the two older brothers? Well, they went away to other countries, which was good riddance, I must say, and no one ever heard of them again.

BRAVE IN SPITE OF
HIMSELF

ONCE upon a time there lived a poor tailor
—and a very poor tailor, indeed—who
worked from morning till night stitching one
thing or another to keep a roof over his head and

food in his mouth. But he dreamed dreams, did this little tailor, and fine dreams they were, too, of dragons and serpents all slain by his hand, and of himself coming home all covered with glory.

And so one day he said to his neighbor the blacksmith, "I wish I were more than a tailor. I wish I could go out into the wide world wearing a helmet and sword made of gold, and killing serpents and monsters."

"Well," said the blacksmith, "that's easily done. There's many a hero needed in this world."

The little tailor shook his head. "I have no money, and 'tis but a short trip you'll make without it," he said. "But I know one thing. I possess the lion's courage, and the strength of a bear. Not even blood can frighten me. Why, I prick my finger every day and feel neither fear nor pain!"

"Indeed you are brave," said the blacksmith. "And I will help you. I have but two gold pieces, yet one of them shall be yours. A gold piece can sparkle for a long time in the hands of a prudent man. Come, take it, and be on your way." And he held out one of his two gold pieces.

Still the little man hesitated. "My wife will be lonely," he said.

"We will care for your wife," said the blacksmith, "your other neighbors and I."

And with this, the tailor was persuaded to go, and he shouted and slapped the table. "When I strike, I strike hard," he cried, and he lifted his hand, and lo and behold, he had killed seven flies at one blow. "Well, see what I have done already," he exclaimed. "Seven at one blow!"

"Remarkable, remarkable indeed!" said the blacksmith. "Now, make a belt and sew across it in big red letters, 'Seven at one blow.' This will tell everyone how strong you are, which, of course, is very important."

The little man followed his friend's advice, and in the afternoon he started out to win power and glory. On his way he met a soldier home from the wars, and from him he bought an old sword for a farthing. And on his way he ate and slept well, too, for a farthing, better than ever he had done as a tailor, for people saw his belt and thought he was already a hero.

But nowhere did he find any dragons to slay or serpents to kill. People had heard of them, yes, but they were always in another country, not in their peaceful kingdom.

Then the little tailor heard of a country called Franconia, and here, it was said, were many dangerous beasts that destroyed the crops and killed the people, leaving no one safe, not even the kings. In fact, they preferred kings best of all, so juicy and fat did they usually find them.

"Well," said the little tailor, "this is just the country for me," and he set out for it on the run.

Several days later he reached the kingdom, and no sooner had he set foot in the land than he was spied by two handsome lads who saw the letters on his belt and hurried him off to the king.

"You are just the man for us," said the king. "We are all heroes here, but there is always room for one more, and plenty of brave deeds for everyone to perform."

"That is good news," said the little tailor, "for I am never happy unless I am slaying dragons or serpents and suchlike creatures. In fact, I don't sleep or eat well if I haven't had a bit of such sport."

"Well then," said the king, "we have just the task for you. In the forest dwell two giants. None of my heroes have been able to kill them, and they have devoured the crops and will soon destroy the country. It will be an easy matter for you to kill them, I am sure, and as a reward, you shall not only sleep and eat well, but you shall win a hundred gold pieces besides."

The little tailor threw out his chest and beat his old rusty sword. "Two giants are nothing," he cried. "Remember I have killed seven at one blow."

To this, everyone nodded with great respect, and then the tailor was conducted to the royal pantry where the queen made ten dainty sandwiches for him with her own fine hands, five filled with jelly and five with the king's best cheese.

Then the little fellow started on his way, and he walked and he walked, and he walked some more, but never a bit of a giant did he see. So he decided to sit down and rest and have a taste of the queen's fine sandwiches.

But no sooner had he taken one bite than there was a fearful stir in the forest, and down trampled two giants so big they could have used the little tailor's own house for a footstool. And at sight of them the brave tailor was no longer brave. He was too frightened to lift a finger, and he cried to himself, "Oh, dear, why didn't I stick to my stitching? Now I am truly lost."

And lost he was, for one of the giants picked him up light as a feather, and holding him by the collar exclaimed, "A nice bit for supper we've found here! We'll chop him up fine and season him with salt."

"No indeed," cried the other giant. "Why, he

is so dry and shriveled he would taste like shoe leather. No indeed, we'll not eat him. We'll hang him and stretch him and then we'll cut him into bow string."

"But I say we will eat him," said the first.

"And I say we will stretch him," said the second, and as they could not agree, they dropped the little tailor, and the first one struck the second a blow with his fist, and the second one tore up a young tree and lashed the first. And then a battle began, and what a battle! They breathed fire and whipped at each other like hurricane winds, and all about them, the forest was tossed up like matchsticks.

Meanwhile the little tailor stood there looking at them, too frightened to move, thinking each moment would be his last, and wishing he were back home with his wife and his stitching.

But finally all was still. The two giants had killed each other dead as a herring and lay there in the midst of the broken trees, and the little tailor, safe now again, regained his courage and climbed up and down the fallen foe, pulling the beard of one, tugging at the leg of the other.

"What a clever fellow I was not to run away," he said at last, and then thrusting his sword through each of the giants, he wiped it off, washed his hands, and sat down to enjoy the rest of the queen's cheese and jelly sandwiches.

And when he returned to the palace with news that the giants were dead, what a fuss everyone made over him! The queen baked him a cake with raisins and almonds, he slept in a bed of real eider down, and the king, himself, polished the gold coins with which he rewarded him.

But one so brave as the little tailor was not to be petted and pampered forever. Across the river dwelt a terrible unicorn with fiery eyes and hooves sharp as knives. He had destroyed the country for miles around and soon would destroy the people, and so the king said to the little tailor, "If you will kill this frightful unicorn, I will pay you a hundred gold pieces, and you shall sleep and eat like a prince."

"I will kill him," said the little tailor, for he had forgotten that he had not really killed the giants, and he longed for more glory. "I will kill him in a trice." And with his head up and his rusty sword clanking at his side, he strode from the palace.

The ferryman took him across the river and left him alone on the edge of a forest. Then he cut through the trees, whistling a tune and clanking his sword merrily. But after a time, the forest grew dark and damp, and a terrible fright came over the tailor.

"Oh, dear," he cried. "Why did I not stick to my stitching? 'Tis better to live with nothing than die for a hundred gold pieces. I will turn back, indeed I will." And he set square about in the opposite direction.

But he got not a step homeward, for at that moment, down through the woods came the terrible unicorn, his fiery eyes lighting the gloom, his sharp hooves cutting the earth, and his one long horn pointed straight at the little tailor's heart. There was no time to run away, it was no use to fight, and so the little tailor fainted dead away and fell to the ground. This sent the unicorn galloping past and straight into a tree, where his horn stuck fast, and the horrible creature's neck was broken.

When the tailor came to again, very much surprised to find himself still alive, there beside him lay the dead unicorn.

"Well!" he exclaimed. "What a clever fellow I was to fall in a faint at sight of that unicorn." And full of boldness once more, he took out his sword and ran it through the animal.

Then he returned to the palace to report his brave deed. And what a great fuss there was in the town this time! All the bells of the city cracked themselves with ringing, and the queen burned herself cooking goodies in the kitchen, and the royal princess kissed the little man on both cheeks.

Now, however, the tailor began to think that he had had enough of honor and of gold, for after all, he was a *very* little fellow, and gold, if not honor, is heavy indeed. So that evening before he went to bed, he stuffed his gold in his knapsack, and in the morning, before the king and queen had washed their faces and put on their crowns, he came to bid them good-bye.

"But you cannot leave us yet," cried the king. "There is one more task that you must perform." And he looked so distressed that the little tailor forgot the heaviness of his gold, and the weariness of his honor, and he said, "Very well, what is the task?"

"A fierce wild boar with bristles like needles and tusks like swords lives in the woods that border our country. He has destroyed everything in sight and will soon destroy us. Now if you will slay that terrible creature, I will give you three hundred pieces of gold, and make you an honorary prince besides."

"That will be easy indeed," said the tailor, for what was one boar to a fearless fellow who had killed seven at one blow, and run his sword through two giants and one unicorn? And to be called His Highness, the Honorary Prince of Franconia, that was an honor not to be overlooked, particularly when he got back home among his rich neighbors. They had always been Master This and Master That while he had been merely the tailor, but now they would be plain This and That, while he was His Highness, the Honorary Prince Tailor.

And so the little tailor set out on his last journey to the far borders of the country to kill the wild boar. But he was followed, alas, by the king and a hundred heroes, for they did not feel safe out of his sight, and this, of course, complicated matters considerably. "Oh, dear," cried the little fellow. "I shall never be able to fall in a faint with the king and all his heroes looking on, and so the boar will surely kill me. Why didn't I stick to my stitching? 'Tis better to be a live tailor than a dead prince." And he moaned and groaned to himself as he marched closer and closer to his doom.

But halfway to the border, the king's bravest duke had a splendid idea. "Your majesty," he said to the king, "I do not think we should endanger your life by following the little tailor any farther. Let us stop here and send him on by himself. He can tell us about the fight afterwards, for he has a fine tongue in his head."

And to this the king agreed, and so he and his hundred heroes with their glittering helmets and armor all stopped and sat down in the shade of the trees and the little tailor and his rusty sword went on alone.

But nothing could have pleased him better, for now he was terribly frightened and wanted only to escape the whole country. "I will wait until the king and his men are out of sight," he exclaimed. "And then I will run across the border, and the king can kill his own animals, and keep my gold, and my honorary prince's title. I will return home a wiser man, if not a richer one, and hereafter, I shall keep my dreams for sleeping."

So he walked bravely ahead until he was lost to sight among the trees, and then he took off his shoes so as to make no sound, and ran quickly and softly through the forest towards the border of Franconia.

He ran till he was out of breath, and out of danger, too, he thought, when what should he hear but a fearful creaking and snorting, and what should he see but a great boar tearing straight towards him through the forest, its bristles cutting the trees like ribbons, and its long tusks scarring the earth.

"Oh, heavens!" cried the little tailor. "Now it's good-bye to this world!" But at that moment, he saw a little stone chapel ahead, and sprinting towards it, he dashed inside. He had no chance to close the door, however, and so the fiery, panting boar rushed in at his heels, and as he jumped from pew to pew, the boar jumped after him, his breath growing hotter and hotter.

At last the little tailor could run no longer. "Well, if I must die," he cried, "I'll save them

the trouble of carrying me to the church," and
he made ready to give up and let the boar devour
him. At that moment, however, he saw an open
window before him, and through this he jumped,
leaving the boar behind. Then he sprinted around
to the front door and closed and bolted it from
the outside. Now the boar was locked in the
church, and the little tailor, safe once more,
straightened himself, and went proudly back to
the king.

"I did not bother to kill the boar," said the
tailor putting his nose in the air. "Such an un-
important creature is too small for my trusty
sword. I merely threw him into the chapel you
will find yonder in the woods, and you and your
men can enjoy the sport of killing him. As for
me, with your leave, I will take my gold and
my honorary prince's title and return home."

"Your wish is granted at once," said the king,
and he dubbed him Honorary Prince Tailor and
then weighted him down with gold and sent
him on his way.

After a long and weary trip, he reached home again. But as he was entering his house, he heard a fearful scream and the sound of beating. In he rushed, and there saw his wife in the hands of a cruel neighbor who was beating her and crying, "That worthless little tailor will never return to you. Now I will beat you until you promise to marry me."

How this angered the Honorary Prince who could kill seven at one blow. "I am returned," he cried. "And I am a great and powerful man, an honorary prince, no less. I have killed seven at one blow, plus two giants, a unicorn, and a wild boar, and now I will kill you, you wretch, if you do not get out!"

And out the man went, meek as a mouse, and the little tailor dropped his sword and took his wife in his arms.

"My, how you frightened that man with your tall tales," said his wife. "And how worn and baggy your clothes look."

"Well," said the little tailor, "the life of a

hero is hard, and money is heavy." And then he showed her all the gold pieces he had with him, and told her his tales of adventure. And now, of course, she believed him, for gold pieces are not to be doubted.

And the tailor became a wealthy man with servants and carriages and silver thimbles to use when he wished to sew a stitch or two. And his good neighbor, the blacksmith, became wealthy, too. And they all lived happily ever after.

THE PRINCESS WHO
ALWAYS BELIEVED
WHAT SHE HEARD

O NCE upon a time, there was a king who
had an only daughter. Now she was young
and fair, and sweet and kind, but she had one
unfortunate fault. She always believed everything she heard, and that would never do, for

there's many a falsehood floating about this great world, particularly in circles of state, and a princess must always know true from untrue. Finally the king proclaimed that anyone who could make his daughter say, "It's a lie," should have her hand in marriage and rule half the kingdom.

Well, what an easy thing all the courtiers thought this would be, for they had long practiced the art of twisting the truth! And so they all vied with each other to tell the princess such lies that even a servant girl would have blushed with shame to believe them. But not a word of protest did the princess make.

When a prince of high repute said, "The moon is made of green cheese," she answered with a sweet sigh, "How I should like to have it for lunch—sliced very thin, of course."

And when a duke of distinction said, "I can balance myself on the head of a pin," she answered prettily, "A remarkable juggler indeed!"

And so on and on it went, till all the courtiers

had tried in vain, and then all the rich merchants' sons took their turn, and as they were
even more skilled than the courtiers in the art
of telling untruths, they each expected to win
the fair princess.

But they had bad luck, too, and it looked as
if the kingdom would go to rack and ruin when
the king died and there was no one to rule but a
princess who could not tell right from wrong.

Then one sunny day, word of the king's plight
reached the end of the kingdom where there
lived a poor woodcutter and his only son, Claus.
Claus was well known for stretching the truth,
and when he heard the news, he said to himself,
"I'm just the lad for the princess," and then and
there he put on his Sunday best, bid his parents
good-bye, and hurried off to the palace.

The king put no faith in the lad, however.
"What would a poor lad like you, living far from
court and understanding little of the ways of the
world, know about true and untrue?" he asked.

"Oh, we country folk are clever," boasted the

lad. "I, myself, am well known for stretching the truth."

"Well, you may try then," said the king. "But where courtiers and merchants' sons have failed, I do not expect a common man to win."

"Well, we shall see what we shall see," said Claus, and so he was introduced to the princess, and they went to walk in the kitchen gardens. Here there were cabbages growing, and by one of them Claus stopped and said, " 'Tis a large cabbage you have here."

"The king feeds many mouths," answered the princess.

"But your cabbages are nothing to compare with my father's," said Claus. "Once we were building a new barn and there were sixteen carpenters working on it. But all of a sudden a storm came up, and it rained so hard that they ran for shelter under one of the cabbage leaves. Then, after a long time, one of the men poked his knife through the leaf to see if the storm was over, and so much water poured through that all the poor men were drowned in an instant."

"What a huge cabbage indeed!" said the princess, and that closed the subject of cabbages.

But the young man was not to be disposed of in this way. He walked the princess over to the palace barn, and he said, " 'Tis a good-sized barn you have here, and solidly built, too."

"A royal house must have a royal barn," said the princess.

"But this barn is nothing compared to my father's barn," boasted Claus. "Why, our barn is so immense that it takes a cow years and years to walk through it from one end to the other. In fact, she comes out so old, she is good for nothing but the glue factory."

"A large barn indeed!" said the princess mildly, and that was the end of the barn.

But it was not the end of Claus, and he walked the princess to the pasture where the king's sheep were grazing.

" 'Tis fine, fat sheep you have, and woolly, too," said the lad.

"The king must sleep warm of a winter's night," said the princess.

"But these sheep are nothing to compare with my father's sheep," said Claus. "Why, their tails are so large that we must tie them to heavy wagons to hold them up, and when the village wants a pot of good soup, all we need to do is cut off a bit of a tail and there is enough for a hundred people. And that is not all! When these sheep are sheared, we have to hire sixteen wood-cutters to chop off the wool with axes, and each sheep takes a month and a day."

"What big sheep indeed!" said the princess, and that was the end of that.

And it would have been the end of Claus, too, were he a courtier or a merchant's son. But the son of a woodcutter was not to be daunted by such a little thing as a wrong-minded princess, so he led her to the king's chicken coops, and here he said, "You grow beautiful chickens, so snowy white, and full of fine cackling, too."

"The king's chickens have something to crow

about," said the princess.

"But they are not so fine as my father's," said the boy. "Why, their feathers are so stiff and long that they can be used for ships' masts, and their eggs are so large they will make a meal for the whole village, and then we can saw the shells in half and there we will have two seaworthy boats. There's nothing slow about the way our hens lay either—ten wagonloads a day, piled high as a castle wall, sometimes even higher, if we don't keep our eyes open. Why, one day we had a pile that reached up to the moon, and I was on top of it. 'Well,' thought I, 'I'll soon climb down,' but before I could make a move, the load toppled over, and there was I, hanging onto the moon, with nothing underneath. And I would have been hanging there still, if I hadn't been a quick-witted lad and found a cobweb that I fastened to a tree and used as a rope so as to lower myself slowly downward. But the cobweb did not reach far enough, alas, and so I had to jump the last few miles. And where should I land but right in the middle of the church! The pastor was taking up a collection for the poor, and your father was there, sitting on the floor with an old nightcap on his head and his pockets stuffed with gold and silver. But when the plate came to him, he refused to give more than one piece of money to the poor. He stuck his nose in the air, that selfish old fellow—"

"Stop!" cried the princess. "It's a lie!" And her pretty face was scarlet with anger. "If you must know," she exclaimed haughtily, "my father never wears anything less than his best crown in the church, and he is not selfish. He has shared many a palace crumb with the poor."

"I daresay that is so," said Claus, the woodcutter's son. "But little does it matter, for I've made you say, 'It's a lie!' and now we'll be wed in the finest style."

This the princess could not deny, and so they were married with great pomp and splendor. And neither Claus nor anyone else ever told lies again—which was very right, of course, but sometimes a little dull, and set Claus to yawning. And once he yawned so wide that he almost swallowed a whole house and lot. But that, of course, is another story!

HANS HUMDRUM

THERE was once a man who had a wife, a farm, and three small sons. The first son was named Peter, the second one Paul, and the last Hans, though he was nearly always called Hans Humdrum because everyone thought he was a little stupid.

Now the farmer was very poor, and so, as the boys grew up, they were sent out into the world to shift for themselves. Since Peter was the oldest, it was his turn to go first, and early one morning his mother gave him a loaf of bread and some butter, and he started on his way.

He had walked hardly a mile, however, when whom should he meet but a rich farmer driving along in fine style. The farmer stopped and he stopped, and the farmer said to him, "Where are you going, my boy?"

"Out to seek my fortune," said Peter.

"Then you have crossed the right path," said the farmer, "for I am in need of a young man like you. Would you care to come and serve me?"

"I would indeed," said Peter, "provided the wages are good enough."

"The wages are fair as fair," said the farmer. "A bushel of dollars for six months' work from now until the first cuckoo calls. But before you say yes, I must warn you that I expect my hired men to be hard working and obedient. They must be up in the morning when the cock crows and work till I tell them to stop."

"You will find me up at the crack of dawn," said Peter. "And I will work like a house afire."

"Very well," said the farmer. "But that is not all. I am a happy, cheerful man, and I do not like to have sour faces around me, so I make an agreement with my hired men that the first one of us who becomes angry shall have a sound thrashing. If I become angry first, I will pay the man his wages, and he may go, so much the richer. But if he is ill-tempered first, I give him no more than his whipping, and out he goes, so much the poorer."

Now Peter considered this a very strange agreement, so he thought it over before saying yea or nay. The farmer looked anything but cheerful, for he was the ugliest man Peter had ever seen. His eyes were tiny, no bigger than a shoe button, his mouth reached from ear to ear, and his nose was so long he could almost stumble over it. But still and all, the wages were nothing to be sneezed at, and as Peter considered himself a good-natured lad and not easily offended, he finally said yes, and agreed to work for the farmer. Then he climbed into the carriage, and away they went, riding in fine style toward the farmer's house.

It was evening when they arrived, and the master told Peter he must begin threshing first thing in the morning. Then he sent the lad to bed, and as it was late, he soon fell fast asleep.

Next morning at six the cock crowed, and in a flash Peter was up and out to the threshing, where he worked for more than an hour without stopping. Then he began to feel hungry, and he wondered when his master would call him to breakfast. But never a sound came from the big farmhouse, so on he worked another hour and still another, until he was too hungry to thresh one more kernel of grain. Then he put down his flail, and walking across the yard, entered his master's house.

Here sat the farmer, and his wife, and his many children, all looking as if they had just enjoyed a fine breakfast, but not a morsel of food was in sight.

"Are you hungry, Peter?" asked the farmer, winking and blinking and twinkling his eyes.

"Yes, of course I am hungry," cried Peter. "I had no supper last night and no breakfast this morning, and well I need food, for I have been threshing these last three hours."

"Look above the door, Peter," said the farmer who, truth to tell, was not really a farmer at all, but a dreadful troll. "Look above the door and see what is written there."

Peter looked, and what should he see but a sign that said, "No breakfast till tomorrow." This provoked the lad, but he well remembered the troll's agreement, so when the old fellow asked, "Are you angry, Peter?" he answered, "Indeed I am not angry," and went whistling back to the barn. Here, fortunately, he found some bread and butter left over from yesterday,

and as he ate it, he said to himself, "Well, no
need to worry today, things will be better tomorrow. My master is but putting me to a test."
Then he threshed on till nightfall and went to
bed and to sleep with an empty stomach.

The next day the cock crowed at four o'clock
instead of six. But this did not trouble Peter.
"The earlier we're up, the sooner we'll eat," he
said, and hurrying into his clothes, he ran to his
work in the barn. He threshed for an hour, then
stopped, thinking his master must surely have
breakfast ready by now. But no one called him
in to eat.

He threshed on another hour, and then was
too hungry to work any longer, so he put down
his flail and went into the house. Everything was
just as it had been the day before. There sat the
master, and his wife, and his many children, all
looking as if they had had a wonderful breakfast, but nowhere in sight was there a morsel
for Peter.

The farmer grinned with his big mouth that

ran from ear to ear, and he said, "Surely you are not hungry, Peter?"

"Indeed I am hungry," answered Peter. "Yesterday I had nothing to eat, and this morning I have worked two long hours without a crumb of food. I am very hungry. I am starved."

The farmer went on grinning. "Look at the writing above the door, Peter," he said. Peter looked up, and there he saw the very same words he had seen the day before, "No breakfast till tomorrow."

"This is tomorrow," cried Peter. "And I am tired of your foolishness. One cannot work without eating."

"And one should not forget his agreements," said the farmer. "You are angry, aren't you, Peter?"

Angry! Yes indeed, for this was no way for a master to treat his servants.

Then how the troll did laugh, and in less time than it can be told, Peter received a sound thrashing, and was tossed outside the gate, sore and bruised, and hardly able to walk away. It took him many days to get home, and then he was obliged to stay in bed for many more. And what was worse, his parents gave him no sympathy whatever. No doubt his master had only wished to put him to a test, they said, and for a bushel of dollars, he should have been willing to go hungry a week.

The parents then sent Paul out to seek his fortune, and early one morning away he started. He traveled a mile or so, and then whom should he meet but the same old troll farmer driving along as before in fine fashion.

"Where are you going, my lad?" asked the farmer.

"Out to seek my fortune," said Paul.

"Then you have crossed the right path, for I am in need of a young man like you," said the farmer. "Would you care to come and serve me?"

"I would indeed," said Paul, "provided the wages are fair enough."

The wages were fair as fair, a bushel of dollars for six months' work from now until the first cuckoo called. But before Paul said yes, he must know that the farmer liked only helpers who were obedient and hard working, and since he was also a very cheerful man, they must be cheerful, too. The farmer explained the agreement he always made with his men, that whoever was angry first should receive a sound thrashing and lose his wages to boot.

It was a strange agreement, Paul thought, but as he was a cheerful lad, he did not worry about it overlong. He said yes, he would work for the farmer, and so off they went at once, driving together in fine style toward the farmer's house.

They arrived at nightfall, and the farmer reminded Paul that he must be up when the cock crowed in the morning and work till he was told to stop. All this Paul promised to do, and then, as it was very late, he went straight to bed and fell fast asleep.

In the morning he was up at the crack of dawn

and went straight to the threshing where he worked for several hours without a moment's stop. Then he began to feel hungry and wondered when the master would call him to breakfast. But never a sound did he hear, and after a time he grew so hungry that he could thresh no longer, so he put down his flail, and went across the yard to the house. There inside sat the farmer, and his wife, and his many children, all looking as if they had just finished a fine meal, but not a morsel of food was in sight for Paul. And when he asked about food, the farmer pointed to the words above the door, "No breakfast till tomorrow."

This provoked Paul, but he remembered the farmer's agreement, so he said, "Very well, master, tomorrow is not far away." And he went whistling back to the barn where, luckily, he found some bread and butter left over from yesterday. This he ate and then went on threshing grain till it was dark and time to go to bed.

The next morning he got up expecting to find

a big breakfast waiting for him, but everything was just the same as the day before, and he worked from dawn to dark with not a bite to eat nor a sip to drink. The same thing happened the third day, too, and then Paul lost his patience, and when the farmer said, "But surely you are not angry, Paul!" he cried, "Indeed I am angry. For three days I have worked from dawn to dark, but not once have I had a bite to eat or a sip to drink. I am angry to bursting."

"Well, that is a sad state of affairs," said the farmer, "for you remember our agreement." Then quick as a wink poor Paul got his thrashing and found himself outside the farmer's gate. He was bruised and sore, and it took him many days to return home, and many more in bed before he was well again.

Now the poor old folks had two sons to take care of and none to seek his fortune, for they did not think Hans Humdrum could be sent out into the world alone. But Hans was of another mind, and while his parents nursed the two older boys and cursed the cruel master, he did a good bit of thinking. Then one morning, without saying a word to anyone, he slipped out of the house and up the highway, bent on making his fortune, too.

He traveled a mile or so, and then, as luck would have it, he also met the old troll farmer with his long nose and his mouth that reached from ear to ear.

"Where are you going, my lad?" asked the farmer.

"Out to seek my fortune," said Hans.

"Then you have crossed the right path, for I am in need of a young man like you," said the farmer. "Would you care to come and serve me?"

"I would indeed," said Hans, "provided the wages are fair enough."

"The wages are fair as fair," said the farmer. "A bushel of dollars for six months' work from now until the first cuckoo calls. But you must be up in the morning with the cocks, and work till I tell you to stop. And I must warn you, too, that I am a cheerful man," said the farmer, and he went on to tell Hans the agreement he always made with his helpers.

"I am cheerful myself," said Hans when the farmer had finished. "And I know we will get along well together."

"Well, we shall see," laughed the farmer grinning from ear to ear. "Now hop into my wagon and we will be off."

This Hans did, and away they went, driving at a fast pace toward the master's farm. They arrived there late that evening and Hans went straight to bed and soon was fast asleep in the very room where his brothers had slept before him.

At six o'clock next morning the cock crowed, and Hans got up and went straight to the threshing. He worked for an hour, then stopped, expecting breakfast to be called. But not a sound came from the big house, so he went in to look for himself. There at the table sat the farmer,

and his wife, and his many children, all looking
as if they had just eaten a fine meal, but not a
morsel was to be seen for Hans.

"Good morning," said the lad politely. "It is
time for breakfast, is it not?"

"I wouldn't say that," said the farmer. "Have
you read what is written above the door?"

Hans looked up and saw the same old sign,
"No breakfast till tomorrow."

"Well, tomorrow is far ahead," he said. "We
can't worry about that until the time comes.
Meanwhile I am a hungry lad."

"Then you may look to the rye for your
food," laughed the farmer, and he sent Hans
flying back to the grain. Here the poor lad
worked on through the morning, saying nothing, but thinking much, and when dinnertime
came, he filled a sack with rye and carried it to an
innkeeper who lived near by.

"My master and I have agreed that I shall not
eat at his house," said Hans, "but I am to look to
the rye for my food. Will you feed me for this

bushel of rye?"

"That I will do, and gladly," said the inn-keeper, and there and then he served Hans a fine dinner, and filled his knapsack for the morrow. This made the lad feel better, and he soon was able to return to his work.

Several days passed in this fashion, and when the farmer asked Hans, "You are not angry, my lad?" he answered promptly, "And why should I be angry? I work well, and you have promised to give me breakfast in the morning."

On the fourth morning, when the farmer had again inquired, "You are not angry, Hans?" and Hans had replied, "Indeed I am not angry," the farmer continued, "But you have had nothing to eat for three whole days, and tomorrow never comes."

"But I have eaten," said Hans, "and well, too, thank you, for I followed your instruction to look to the rye for my food, and each day I ex-change a bushel of rye with the innkeeper for a fine dinner and other provisions besides."

At this, the farmer's eyes almost bulged out of his head and his long mouth fell down to his chin.

"I hope master is not angry with me," said Hans innocently.

"By no means," said the farmer, trying very hard to look cheerful again. "But now you have done enough threshing and I have another task for you. I want you to plow some of the fields. My dog will go with you, and when he lies down you must start, and when he gets up you must stop, and if he comes home you must follow, no matter the path he may take."

Hans did as his master ordered, and when the dog lay down, he started to plow and worked till noon without stopping. Then he began to feel hungry, and he looked inquiringly at the dog. But that creature seemed in no hurry to leave, so he seized a whip and struck him soundly across the legs. At that, the dog was quite willing to go, and leaping up with a howl, he streaked across the field toward home. Hans then jumped

down from the plow, undid the horses, and
rode after the dog at a furious pace.

When they reached the house, the dog jumped
over the garden fence, and Hans jumped the
horses after him. However, they were not as
nimble as the dog, and one of them fell and broke
his leg, while the other one ran into a fence post.
Neither could move now, and when the troll
farmer ran out of his house and saw what had
happened, he looked black as thunder.

But Hans said with a smile, "Surely you are
not angry, master, for I was only obeying your
orders. I am not to blame if the horses cannot
jump over the fence as nimbly as a dog."

"I am not angry," said the troll. "Come in and
have some dinner," and he tried very hard to
smile from one end of his big mouth to the other.
But it was difficult, for he was beginning to fear
this boy who obeyed him so completely.

Hans had both dinner and supper, and the
next morning the troll sent him out to tend the
pigs. There were fifty of them, sleek and fat,

and just ready for market.

"Let them go wherever they wish," said the troll. "Let them bury themselves in the mud if that's what they want."

"Yes indeed, master," said Hans, and he followed the pigs out of the yard.

The animals wandered slowly up the road, eating here and there, and Hans idly followed them until he met a couple of men who had been about the countryside buying cattle and swine.

"What fine pigs you have there," said the men to Hans.

"The best from here to yonder and back again," replied Hans.

"And would you be willing to sell them?" asked the men.

"I would indeed," answered Hans, "for a fine pig looks better on the table than on the hoof. I will sell all but this big one," and he pointed to an old sow. "She is intended as a present for the pastor."

"What a good lad to think of the pastor," said

the buyers, and so they paid Hans well for the pigs, and a dollar extra besides. Then they drove east with their fine, fat swine, and Hans walked west with his one lone sow. He had his eye out for a marsh, and when he came to one, he let the pig bury herself in the mud until only her tail stood above the ground. Then he returned to the house.

"What has become of my pigs?" cried the troll when he saw that Hans was all alone.

"Master, master," Hans replied, "your pigs rooted themselves into the bog and all are lost except one old sow. I hung onto her tail and that is still above the mud, but all the rest are gone."

The troll shrieked and ran down to the bog. There he saw the tail of his one poor pig waving above the mud, and he reached down and tried to pull her out. But the tail slipped between his fingers, and down he, too, tumbled into the bog. When he pulled himself out again, wet and muddy, Hans said, "I hope you are not angry with me, master. I did only what you said to do."

"No, I am not angry," said the troll, but he did not smile, and he ran wildly about, looking for his lost pigs, which, alas, he could not find, for as Hans had explained, they were now far away.

Finally he gave up and went home, and when he saw his wife, he said, "What can I do to get rid of that wretched boy before he does away with everything I own? If only I could tell him how angry I am! Why did I make that foolish agreement?"

"Never fear," cried his wife. "We can easily get rid of him. He knows that his time is up when the first cuckoo calls, so we will play a trick on him. You cover me with tar and roll me in feathers till I look like a bird. Then help me up into the large apple tree, and there I will cry, 'Cuckoo, cuckoo,' until Hans thinks that the bird has really come and you can send him sailing."

"My, but you are a clever woman," exclaimed the troll, and he grinned for the first time in many days. "I will do exactly as you say." And with that he made ready for tomorrow's trick.

The next morning as Hans and the troll sat at the table eating breakfast, they heard the loud call of a cuckoo.

"Well, what a surprise," exclaimed the troll. "I do believe the cuckoo has come."

"Then I must see him," cried Hans. "I have always wanted to have a look at the first summer cuckoo." And he jumped up and ran outside to the garden. There he saw the strangest-looking bird he had ever laid eyes on in all his life, and picking up a sharp stone, he threw it straight at the creature's head. Down she fell, stone dead, and Hans cried to the troll, "Come, master, come and look at this strange bird."

Now of course it was not really a bird that Hans had killed, but the troll's old woman, and when he rushed out and saw what had happened, he was so angry that sparks flew from his eyes and his voice roared like thunder.

"I hope master is not angry," said Hans softly.

"Indeed I am angry," cried the troll. "You have sold my rye, you have ruined my horses, and lost my swine, and now you have killed my wife. I could tear you limb from limb, you scoundrel." And he shook like a hurricane, he was so full of rage and fury.

"Well," said Hans quietly, "that is indeed sad, for now I must deal with you according to the terms of our agreement." And he seized the troll and thrashed him until the old fellow could not lift a finger. Then he ran gaily into the house, took the bushel of dollars which was due him and returned home to his parents and brothers. And here they all lived happily ever after, and neither saw nor heard any more of the troll.